DISCOVER THE GIFT OF JOY

DISCOVER THE GIFT OF JOY

HOW TO EXPERIENCE JOY IN LIFE, WORK AND RELATIONSHIPS

SHAJEN JOY AZIZ

ISBN: 979-8-9954964-1-0 (Paperback)
ISBN: 979-8-9954964-3-4 (Hardcover)

"If you're holding back the Gift, then what you're asking is for other people in the world to hold back their Gifts from you. The more you give your Gift, the more you participate and make a difference in the world, the more the world will make a difference for you."

– Sonia Powers

Our *Discover the Gift of Joy: Journal & Coloring Book* takes you through each of The Eight Steps of discovery. With more extensive guided meditations, it's the perfect addition for your deep reflections and personal journey to joy.

Find it at amazon.com.

About Publishing Joy

Shajen Joy Aziz, M.Ed., M.A. Award-Winning #1 International Best-Selling Author, Speaker, Publisher & Educator

Shajen is a global leader in transformational storytelling and personal development. With advanced degrees in Education and Psychology and over 28 years of experience, she empowers authors, thought leaders, and visionaries to find their voice, own their story, and bring their message to the world with clarity and confidence. As the co-founder of Publishing Joy and co-creator of *Discover the Gift*, her work bridges science and soul – helping individuals turn their stories into powerful platforms for impact.

I thank Kim Somers Egelsee for helping me get the publishing company off the ground. Her time at Publishing Joy was instrumental to our success. Here is a little bit about her:

Kim Somers Egelsee is an intuitive, TEDx speaker, 14x best-selling author, co-founder of Publishing Joy, life, business, marketing and speaking coach and podcast host. For over 20 years, she has specialized in helping people exude confidence, connect authentically and discover their life's purpose. She gives them a platform to shine their unique gifts through writing, speaking and media.

Kim holds a degree in Speech Communication, as well as credentials in Educational Psychology, from CSULB. She is certified in hypnotherapy, NLP, energy healing and Life Coaching. Kim has led and spoken at over 500 events, workshops and masterminds.

www.publishing-joy.com

CONTENTS

ACKNOWLEDGMENTS

First and foremost, we offer our deepest gratitude to the original creators of *Discover the Gift*, the core group who brought this work into being and into the world. This foundation was created alongside **David Hagen**, **Cherif Aziz**, **Shajen Joy Aziz** and **Demian Lichtenstein**, without whom none of this would be possible.

Together, these four stepped into something far greater than any one individually, diving deeply into the creation of the documentary, into the production of the work, and into the unfolding of what the world now knows as *Discover the Gift*.

To each of you, thank you. This body of work, and all that continues to emerge from it, exists because of the shared vision, devotion, and willingness to bring something meaningful forward.

From Shajen: A heartfelt thank you to **Random House** for the support and guidance you offered me as a young author. Your influence helped shape not only my understanding of publishing, but my confidence in stepping forward as a voice in this space. That foundation has stayed with me, and I carry that gratitude with great respect.

To **Kim Somers Egelsee**, my incredible partner and dear friend, thank you. Publishing Joy began as a vision, a dream I shared with you, and together, we chose to step into it fully, with intention, courage, and trust. Today, we stand in that vision, bringing forward *Discover the Gift of Joy: How to Experience Joy in Life, Work and Relationships*, alongside the companion journal and coloring book, where soul and science meet in a deeply integrated way.

Thank you for your partnership, your presence, and your unwavering commitment to this mission. You are extraordinary.

From Kim: To my partner, **Shajen Joy Aziz**, I am so grateful we have not only known each other for years, but now we get to create and work together on this extraordinary journey of spreading light throughout the world.

And a heartfelt thank you to **Dr. Barbara De Angelis** for your unwavering support of *Discover the Gift* from its original creation through its continued evolution, and especially for your presence in this book. Your guidance, wisdom, and belief have helped shape what is now unfolding in such a meaningful way. We are deeply grateful, from the bottom of our hearts.

To **Laurel Janssen Byrne**, our co-editor, thank you for your support in the editing process.

To **Connor Belvin**, who co-created the cover of *Discover the Gift of Joy*, thank you for bringing vision into form with such brilliance. What began as a collection of ideas, expressed through a simple collage, was transformed through your artistry into something far beyond imagination.

Each lotus on the cover represents an author, a point of light, sharing wisdom, story, and truth with the world.

You captured that essence beautifully.

A heartfelt thank you to **Paul Heussenstamm** of Mandalas.com for his constant inspiration and beautiful creation of mandalas. His mandalas were featured in the original work of Discover the Gift, the documentary film, and the accompanying book, helping bring beauty, symbolism, and deeper reflection to the experience. The mandalas you will find throughout this book are inspired by his work, his artistry, and his devotion to this sacred form of creative expression.

And to each of our authors, this book exists because of you. Your willingness to share your stories, your insights, and your truth with depth, vulnerability, and courage is what makes this work alive.

You are the heartbeat of this book.

You are the light within it.

Thank you for allowing your voices to be heard, for contributing so meaningfully, and for opening pathways for others to discover joy in new and profound ways.

This is why we are here.

FOREWORD

BY DR. BARBARA DE ANGELIS

This important book has found its way to you at this exact moment on your journey for a reason. I know firsthand both as a life-long seeker and having been an author for over four decades that, at its best, a book is meant to be a sacred doorway, one that beckons you to enter and begin a transformational adventure that has been lovingly and carefully prepared for you. If you are reading this, it means you *are* ready for that adventure, the kind that offers illuminating wisdom that can uplift you, expand you, and awaken your own inner treasures.

Deep in the Center of your being, the immeasurable treasure of your Joy awaits you!

The word 'joy' originates from the Latin root *'gau'* which meant *'to rejoice'*. In contrast, the word 'happiness' is derived from the old English *'hap'*, which meant *"luck"* or *"chance"*. This comparison reminds us that happiness is an emotional response dependent upon positive, outer circumstances that occur through luck, chance, and the unpredictable ever-changing realities of human life, none of which we can ever fully control. Sometimes we feel happy. Sometimes we do not. Certain people and situations give us the experience of happiness, while others cause us to undergo discomfort, agitation, or even suffering.

Joy, however, is an experience that can only rise up from within you. It is an inner rejoicing, independent of the circumstances, challenges, and dramas of your life. It is a return to and immersion in the Bliss that is your spiritual essence at your true Source.

When we find our way back to the Joy within, we recognize it as the very impulse of the Divine, a gift that was always present, there for us to discover it, open to it, and allow it to fill us with a wholeness and fulfillment that nothing and no one can take away from us.

Here is how we can understand the title *"Discover the Gift of Joy."* To discover something means that it *already* exists and is *already* available, that it was never missing and therefore doesn't need to be searched for. This gift is not something that you need to earn or be worthy of. It is yours. It belongs to you. It simply requires your participation so it can be unwrapped and delighted in.

The beautiful lotuses on the cover of this book depict the perfect metaphor for the true meaning of discovering joy. From ancient times and across religions and civilizations, the lotus has been regarded as a mystical symbol of spiritual awakening and rebirth. The lotus flower closes when it gets dark at night, and reopens each morning when it becomes bathed in the radiant light from the Sun. Like the luminous petals of a lotus, Joy is meant to unfold within you as your consciousness becomes increasingly illuminated with wisdom, revelation and remembrance.

May you allow yourself to be transported deep into the enlightening places these pages take you inside of yourself!

May you be guided back to the limitless, overflowing, shimmering source of Joy that awaits you in your True Heart!

May your journey to Joy be graceful, astonishing, and sublime!

May you live with Joy, love from Joy, and serve our world in Joy!

– **Dr. Barbara De Angelis**

#1 NY Times Bestselling Author and Transformational Teacher

April 2026, Santa Barbara, California

Introduction

Discover the Gift of Joy: It's Why We're Here

What an extraordinary journey it has been.

To come home to myself.

To raise my daughter.

To build a life rooted in the quiet beauty of Vermont.

Discover the Gift has always been about presence. About honoring the moments that shape us. About waking up to our choices and the life we are actively creating.

When I reflect on the original *Discover the Gift*, supported by extraordinary legacy authors and contributors from around the world, I am filled with gratitude. That work changed me. It changed everyone it touched.

And yet, the moment that changed everything came unexpectedly.

During a podcast interview, I was asked a question that stopped me completely:

"What did you learn?
Not what I taught.
Not what I shared.
But what I learned."

I was not prepared.

And in that unguarded moment, something honest emerged.

What I learned became the foundation of everything that followed.

Insight.
Intention.
Integrity.
Involvement.

These were not simply ideas.

They became a way of living.

They guided me through my quiet seasons.

Through motherhood.

Through caring for my father.

Through building a life that not only works for me but contributes to a world that works for others.

During this time, I stepped more deeply into my work as a therapist, serving through the Vermont Wellness Collaborative. That journey transformed me. It showed me, again and again, that people can heal. That we hold more within us than we have been told. That it is never too late to choose differently.

And still, I never stopped building *Discover the Gift*.

I continued teaching, consulting, and expanding the work.

And through that evolution, something new began to reveal itself.

A fifth principle emerged.

One that made sense of everything that had come before.

Integration.

Because it is not enough to understand something.

It is not enough to set an intention, or even to act with integrity and involvement.

True transformation happens when we weave what we know into the fabric of how we live. When insight stops being something we visit and becomes something we inhabit.

We now understand, through decades of research in neuroscience and well-being, that when awareness and action are consistently aligned, the brain itself begins to change. New neural pathways form. Resilience deepens. Regulation becomes less effortful, more natural. We move out of survival and into openness. Into clarity. Into compassion. Into choice.

And from that place, something becomes possible that fear had made unreachable.

Genuine connection.

Genuine joy.

What may feel like a small act of care from you can quietly change the entire shape of someone else's day. Or their life.

And here is the truth this work is built on.

The gift is not outside of you.

It is not something distant.

It is not something you must chase or become.

You are the gift.

Your presence.

Your authenticity.

Your willingness to be seen.

The way you share, create, and express. Especially in the unguarded moments, when you are not over-editing or holding yourself back.

Sometimes your gift is as simple as a word. A sentence. A smile offered at exactly the right moment. One that quietly changes everything.

We are walking this earth together. And the smallest acts carry the greatest meaning.

A kind word when silence would have been easier.

A helping hand when it is needed.

The quiet choice to act with integrity, whether anyone is watching or not.

Integrity lives in the grand moments, and it lives in the smallest ones. It is in picking up a piece of trash on a forest path. It is in choosing what brings you peace. It is in honoring the life that feels true for you.

Because it is within your peace that you discover who you truly are.

Not the reactive self.

Not the conditioned self.

But the regulated self.

The integrated self.

The true self.

For me, arriving at that place was a journey.

And it was not always a gentle one.

What I know about transformation, I did not only learn in a classroom or a therapy room.

I lived it.

After my mother passed, my life came apart in ways I had not imagined. There was pain I did not have names for. There were wounds inside my family that required more forgiveness than I thought I had.

And I was learning how to live without her.

Not just in the early days of grief. But in every ordinary moment that followed. The milestones she would not witness. The questions I could no longer ask. The particular silence of a life that has lost its first teacher of love.

What carried me was resilience.

Not the kind that looks strong from the outside. The quiet kind. The kind that simply gets up. That chooses, on the hardest days, to take one more step. That finds a reason, however small, to remain open when every instinct says to close.

I did not always feel resilient. But I chose it. Again and again. In the dark and in the ordinary. In the moments no one saw and the moments I could barely see myself.

And alongside that resilience, there were people.

People who stayed. Who did not look away from my pain or ask me to make it smaller so they could be more comfortable. Who sat with me in the hard places and did not rush me toward the light. Who offered their presence when I had nothing to offer in return.

Those people saved my life.

I do not say that lightly.

They showed me what love looks like when it asks for nothing. They showed me that healing is not something we earn or achieve alone. It is something that happens between people, in the tender space of being truly seen.

We are not meant to heal alone. Something in us requires being witnessed, being held, being part of something larger than our own pain.

And through all of it, through the grief and the rebuilding and the long quiet years of learning how to live without her, one thing never left me.

Joy.

Not the loud kind. Not the kind you perform for others. A small glowing ember that appeared when I least expected it. In the slant of morning light. In my daughter's laugh. In a stranger's kindness. In the way an ordinary moment would suddenly open and remind me that life was still full of sweet surprises.

That ember never went out.

Even in my darkest seasons, it was there. Waiting. Patient. Certain in a way I was not always certain myself.

I still wake up ready to greet the day.

That is not a small thing. That is everything.

And I want you to know something.

It has not left you either.

Whatever you have been through. However long the hard season has lasted. However, many times you have wondered if you would find your way back to yourself.

That ember is still in you.

It did not go out when everything else felt like it did. It was there in the moments you kept going when you had every reason to stop. It was there in the small things that still moved you, even when you thought you were too tired to be moved. It is there right now, in the quiet fact that you are holding this book and you have not given up.

Joy has been waiting for you.

Not somewhere far away. Right here. In you. Patient and certain, the way it has always been.

Over time, I chose to heal.

I chose to grow.

I chose to recreate my life.

And in doing so, I began to generate a world I love living in. One I am honored to share with you

And then, years later, life asked me to heal again.

Not the same wound. A new one.

And in that second season of loss, I did what I had learned to do the first time.

I came back to my own work.

Not as a teacher reviewing her material. But as a student, humbled, starting over. I returned to The Eight Steps the way you return to something you trust when everything else has fallen away. Not because I had all the answers. But because I knew where the door was.

And the door, as it has always been, was Receptivity

The willingness to be open before I was ready.

To receive before I could see what was coming.

To honor the beginning, even when beginning again felt like loss.

That practice carried me. Again. I offer it to you now because I have lived it. Not once. Twice. And it answered me. It will answer you too.

A Moment of Receptivity

Before you go further, pause here.

Place one hand on your heart.

Take one breath in. Let it go slowly.

And ask yourself, gently and without judgment:

What am I ready to receive?

Do not search for the answer. Let it rise.

It may come as a word. A feeling. A memory. An image. A single quiet knowing that has been waiting for you to be still enough to hear it.

Whatever arrives, it is welcome here. You are welcome here.

When you are ready, turn to the mandala on the next page. Let your hands continue what your heart has begun. There are no rules. Only color, breath, and the gift of your own presence.

Joy is not incidental to this work. It is the foundation of it.

Joy is my middle name. It was my mother's middle name. It is an energy that has always guided me. Through grief, through rebuilding, through the quiet seasons and the expansive ones. It is the thread that connects everything I have created, and everything I continue to offer.

And so these two books, *Discover the Gift of Joy* and the journal and mandala coloring book that accompanies it, are not separate offerings.

They are two expressions of the same invitation.

One gives you the story, the science, and the soul of this work. The other asks you to live it. Through reflection, through action, through the sacred practice of putting pen to page and color to image, allowing your own inner wisdom to surface and speak.

And now, beloved, I want to speak directly to you.

You did not arrive here by accident.

Something in you recognized this work before your mind had words for it.

Perhaps you have sensed for a long time that there is more. More depth. More joy. More of yourself waiting on the other side of the stories you have been telling.

You are ready for this.

Not because you have it all together. Not because the hard seasons are behind you. But because you are here, in this moment, willing to open. And that willingness, that single courageous act of showing up, is itself the beginning of everything.

The Eight Steps you are about to experience, and the stories you are about to step into, were written for exactly who you are and exactly where you stand.

The authors gathered in these pages were chosen with intention. Their stories, their wisdom, their voices. Each one carries a gift that belongs in this conversation. Together they offer new ways of seeing joy. New ways of moving through life and receiving all it has to offer.

They were chosen for you. All of it was. Not for who you were.

Not for who you are still becoming. For who you are right now, in this moment, holding this book. That is enough because you are enough.

Love is the ultimate Gift and encompasses everything. It is an endless well that has been here all along, ready for you to receive it. Stay open, you are worth it.

Thank you for being here. Thank you for saying yes to a journey inward and one filled with joy.

It's why we're here.

– SHAJEN JOY AZIZ, M.ED., M.A.

Beginning the Journey of Discovering the Gift of Joy

There are moments in life when something inside of us quietly asks for our attention.

Not urgently or loudly.
Just gently.

It may arrive as a question we cannot ignore. A feeling that there must be something more. Or a quiet realization that, even in the midst of life's challenges, something beautiful is waiting to be noticed. That something is joy.

Not the kind of happiness that comes and goes with circumstances, but a deeper experience that lives within us. It is a steady presence, available even during uncertainty, growth, and transformation.

Many of us spend years searching for happiness outside ourselves. We look for it in achievements, approval, and moments when everything is working out as we hoped. While those moments are meaningful, they are often temporary. Joy is different.

Joy begins to emerge when we recognize that life itself participates in our growth. It is the quiet strength that appears when we begin to trust that even our most difficult experiences may carry insight, wisdom, and unexpected gifts. This understanding is at the heart of the *Discover the Gift* journey.

Years ago, the original book *Discover the Gift: It's Why We're Here* introduced a simple perspective: every life experience has the potential to be a gift. Even our most challenging moments can lead to new awareness, compassion, and strength.

For thousands around the world, the idea became more than a philosophy. It became a way of life. It invited people to pause and reflect differently on their lives. It encouraged looking beyond the surface of events, and asking a new question: What might life be trying to show me here?

As people began exploring this perspective, something remarkable unfolded. What once felt like isolated struggles began to transform into meaningful turning points. Challenges became growth opportunities. Stories that once carried pain began to carry wisdom.

And within that transformation, many people discovered something unexpected. Joy.

Not because life had suddenly become easier, but because their relationship with life had changed. They began to see themselves not as victims of circumstance, but as participants in a living process of learning, evolving, and becoming. This book grows from that realization.

Discover the Gift of Joy explores how resilience, awareness, and compassion allow us to experience joy in ways that are deeper and more sustainable than the fleeting happiness we often chase. Examining current research and knowledge on brain potential, we can see how what we focus on expands in ways that align with our choices.

Modern neuroscience supports what many spiritual traditions have long understood. The human brain is capable of change throughout our lives. Through reflection, awareness, and intentional practice, we can strengthen neural pathways associated with gratitude, meaning, and emotional resilience. This ability, known as neuroplasticity, reminds us that transformation is not only possible; it is also a reality. It is natural.

Each time we pause to reflect, choose compassion over judgment, or learn from an experience, we shape how our minds and hearts respond. In other words, we begin to cultivate joy.

Throughout these pages, you will encounter stories, reflections, and insights that invite you to explore your own life with curiosity and openness. You will see how The Eight Steps of *Discover the Gift* can guide us toward deeper understanding, greater resilience, and a more compassionate relationship with ourselves and others.

You may notice that this book does not ask you to become someone different. Instead, it invites you to remember what has always been within you.

Your capacity for awareness.
Your capacity for growth.
Your capacity for joy.

Acknowledge, recognize, understand, and integrate your recurring themes and life lessons so you can stay connected to your power to change gears, pivot as needed, and stay aligned with your sources of joy. As Janet Attwood teaches us in *Discover the Gift – It's Why We're Here*, "always choose in favor of your passions, they are the breadcrumbs that lead you to your gift." To reflect on yourself and your life experiences and act on your knowing, choosing in favor of the things that bring you happiness and activate joy. The more you follow through on what you know to be true for you in positive ways, the more your life unfolds gracefully.

Life will always bring change. It will continue to offer both challenges and opportunities. Within every experience lies the possibility of insight, if we pause long enough to listen.

This is the beginning of the invitation. An invitation to explore your life with new eyes. An invitation to recognize gifts already unfolding in your experiences. Most importantly, an invitation to rediscover joy that has been waiting within you.

Thank you for beginning this journey. You are worth it, and so are those in your sphere of influence.

The Discover the Gift Perspective

Discover the Gift's philosophy: every experience has the potential for growth and understanding.

When we approach our experiences with awareness and curiosity, we begin to see the lessons life offers. Through reflection, intention, and compassion, we develop qualities that support deeper well-being.

Happiness celebrates moments. Joy grows from how we understand and connect with those moments. Seeing life through this lens opens new possibilities. Joy is not a thing to find, but something we cultivate through awareness, meaning, and love.

Returning to What Has Always Been Within You

There comes a moment in life when something quietly begins to shift. Not all at once, but steadily, like the changing seasons. You notice what no longer fits, aligns, or feels true. Beneath all your noticing, something else emerges. A remembering. Not of something new, but of something old within you. Joy never truly left. It has been waiting beneath the noise, expectations, and patterns you were taught. Waiting for you to return.

Joy is not earned or reserved for certain achievements. It is not a reward. Joy is a state of alignment, a natural expression of who you are when you live in connection with your truth. Yet many people are conditioned to seek it outside themselves. They chase happiness through accomplishment, validation, and outcomes that promise fulfillment, but often something is still missing. Happiness, as often experienced, is responsive to events. Joy is different; it arises from within.

Modern neuroscience offers something both profound and empowering. Your brain is not stuck or set by your past. It is always changing (Doidge, 2007; Davidson & McEwen, 2012). This ability is called neuroplasticity. It means the brain can reorganize itself through experience, attention, and practice. What you repeatedly focus on, feel, or practice is strengthened within (Hebb, 1949; Siegel, 2020). Frequently used neural pathways work better, while others weaken. Over time, these create patterns of thought, emotion, and response. What feels like "just how I am" is often just what's been practiced. What's practiced can be reshaped.

Affective neuroscience shows that emotions are not only temporary states, but become conditioned responses over time (Davidson, 2003; Phelps & LeDoux, 2005). The more often we activate an emotional pathway, the more likely it is to activate again. This explains why stress can become habitual, anxiety automatic, and disconnection familiar. Yet, there's good news. Joy can be learned. Calm can be strengthened. Connection can return. Not by force or denial, but through conscious, repeated experience.

When you experience joy, your brain responds in measurable and meaningful ways. Neurochemicals such as dopamine, serotonin, and oxytocin are released, supporting motivation, mood regulation, and social bonding (Berridge & Kringelbach, 2015; Young, 2009). These are not simply "feel-good" chemicals. They are part of a complex biological system that reinforces learning, connection, and well-being. Each time you experience joy, you are not only feeling something in the moment; you are strengthening the neural pathways that make that experience more accessible in the future. In this way, you are quite literally teaching your brain how to return to that state. This is how joy becomes more than a moment. It becomes a pattern.

Research in positive psychology continues to show that emotions such as joy, love, and contentment play a unique role within the human system. They broaden awareness, expand perception, and increase creativity, openness, and connection (Fredrickson, 2001; 2013). Where stress narrows your focus for survival, joy opens your awareness for possibility. This expansion allows you to build internal and external resources over time, including stronger relationships, greater resilience, and deeper clarity. As these resources develop, joy becomes easier to access. Researchers describe this as an upward spiral of well-being, a self-reinforcing pattern in which positive emotional experiences lead to increased well-being, which in turn makes future positive experiences more likely (Fredrickson & Joiner, 2002).

An important distinction emerges within this understanding. Happiness is often tied to external conditions. It is influenced by circumstances, achievements, and outcomes. Joy, however, is rooted in something deeper. It is connected to meaning, authenticity, and living in alignment with one's values and inner truth. Research on eudaimonic well-being continues to affirm that lasting fulfillment arises not from external success alone, but from living in alignment with who you truly are (Ryan & Deci, 2001; Huta & Waterman, 2014). This is where joy lives. Not in what you acquire, but in what you embody.

One of the most empowering insights from modern neuroscience is that attention shapes the brain. Where you place your focus matters (Siegel, 2007; Hanson, 2013). Practices such as mindfulness, gratitude, intentional reflection, and conscious awareness have been shown to influence emotional regulation and reshape neural pathways over time (Davidson et al., 2003; Goleman & Davidson, 2017). This means your emotional experience is not fixed. You are not at the mercy of your patterns. You are in a relationship with them. And through awareness, intention, and practice, that relationship can change.

You are not here to become someone else. You are here to remember who you are. To release what is misaligned, to recognize what is true, and to reconnect with the essence of your being. Joy is not something missing. It is something often covered. Covered by expectation, by conditioning, and by patterns that once served a purpose but no longer do. As those layers begin to soften, something natural emerges. Not forced or manufactured but revealed.

This book is not asking you to chase joy. It is inviting you to uncover it. To understand the patterns that shape your experience, to become aware of where your attention has been placed, and to begin gently and powerfully directing your life from a place of alignment. The science is clear. The brain changes with experience. Emotions can be reshaped. Patterns can be rewired. And joy is not something outside of you waiting to be found. It is something within you, waiting to be lived.

As you move through this journey, you will begin to see how each step, each awareness, and each experience builds upon the next. This is not about perfection. It is about practice. Not about forcing change but allowing transformation. Not about becoming more but becoming aligned. Because when alignment begins, joy does not need to be created. It begins to emerge naturally, steadily, and powerfully.

Happiness and Joy: Understanding the Difference

People often use the words happiness and joy interchangeably, yet research in psychology and neuroscience suggests they represent two different dimensions of well-being. Understanding this distinction can help us recognize why joy can persist even amid life's challenges.

Happiness: The Experience of Positive Moments

Happiness is often connected to circumstances. It tends to arise when something pleasant happens in our lives. We feel happy when we receive good news, accomplish a goal, enjoy time with loved ones, or experience something beautiful or meaningful.

Psychologists often describe this form of well-being as hedonic well-being, which refers to the experience of pleasure and positive emotion. Hedonic happiness is valuable and important. It allows us to enjoy life's positive moments and celebrate meaningful experiences. However, because it is connected to circumstances, happiness can change depending on what is happening around us.

Happiness often comes and goes with the changing events of life. Yes, that happened, and what did I make it mean about myself? We are meaning-making machines, so our interpretation matters. Joy is a different state of being. It comes from within.

> *"Happiness is not the result of what we get, but of how we interpret and engage with life."*
> – Martin Seligman

Joy: A Deeper State of Meaning and Connection

Joy tends to operate differently. Joy is less dependent on circumstances and more connected to meaning, connection, and inner alignment. Researchers often associate joy with eudaimonic well-being, a form of well-being that arises from living with purpose, authenticity, and engagement with life.

Joy can exist even during times of challenge or uncertainty because it is rooted in a deeper sense of meaning and connection. Psychologist Dr. Barbara Fredrickson, known for her research on positive emotions, explains that positive emotional states expand our awareness and help build long-term psychological resilience.

> *"Positive emotions broaden our awareness and build lasting personal resources."*
> – Barbara Fredrickson

These resources include resilience, creativity, social connection, and emotional strength. Over time, experiences of meaning, gratitude, compassion, and connection help cultivate a deeper sense of well-being that many people describe as joy.

The Neuroscience Perspective

Neuroscience also helps explain why joy can feel more stable than happiness. Our brains are constantly adapting through a process known as neuroplasticity, meaning that repeated thoughts, emotions, and behaviors shape the neural pathways that influence how we experience the world. When we practice reflection, gratitude, compassion, and intentional awareness, we strengthen neural circuits associated with emotional regulation and resilience.

> *"Well-being is a skill that can be cultivated."*
> – Richard Davidson

Practices such as reflection, journaling, meditation, and gratitude help reinforce the neural patterns that support emotional balance and deeper well-being. Over time, these practices can help foster a more stable sense of joy.

Why the Distinction Matters

Recognizing the difference between happiness and joy can change the way we relate to our experiences. Happiness celebrates life's positive moments while joy helps us remain grounded in meaning and connection, even when circumstances are difficult. Both are valuable. Yet joy often becomes the deeper foundation that supports resilience, compassion, and long-term well-being.

> *"When we are no longer able to change a situation, we are challenged to change ourselves."*
> – Viktor Frankl

Meaning allows people to discover purpose even in difficult experiences. And through meaning, joy can emerge.

A Simple Way to Understand the Difference

Happiness often comes from what happens to us. Joy grows from how we understand and connect with our experiences. Happiness celebrates the moment. Joy sustains the journey. When we cultivate awareness, gratitude, compassion, and purpose, we strengthen the qualities that allow joy to become part of our everyday lives. And as we continue to grow awareness, we often discover something remarkable. Joy was never something we needed to chase. It was something we could cultivate from within.

Neuroscience and Psychology, In Simple Terms

While the words happiness and joy are often used interchangeably, psychological research suggests they describe two distinct forms of well-being. Both are valuable, and they both enrich our lives. Yet they arise from various sources and influence us in diverse ways. Understanding this distinction can help us appreciate why joy can remain present even when life is difficult.

Happiness — Hedonic Well-Being

Happiness is often connected to circumstances and experiences. It arises when something positive happens in our lives. We may feel happy when we accomplish a goal, enjoy time with loved ones, receive recognition, or experience moments of beauty and pleasure.

Psychologists describe this form of well-being as hedonic well-being, which focuses on positive emotion and pleasure. Hedonic happiness is an important part of life. It allows us to celebrate success, connection, and enjoyment. However, because it is tied to external experiences, happiness can change as circumstances change.

> *"Well-being comes from meaning, engagement, and connection."*
> – Martin Seligman

Happiness often reflects the positive moments we experience along the journey.

Joy — Eudaimonic Well-Being

Joy tends to arise from deeper sources within our lives. It is connected to meaning, purpose, authenticity, and connection with others. Psychologists refer to this form of well-being as eudaimonic well-being, which focuses on living in alignment with our values and contributing to something meaningful.

Joy can remain present even during life's challenges because it is rooted in understanding and purpose rather than circumstance.

> *"Positive emotions broaden our awareness and build lasting personal resources."*
> – Barbara Fredrickson

Over time, these emotional resources strengthen resilience, creativity, and connection. Joy grows through meaning and awareness.

The Brain and Well-Being

Neuroscience offers additional insight into why practices such as reflection, gratitude, and compassion help cultivate joy. Our brains continually adapt through neuroplasticity, the brain's ability to form and strengthen new neural pathways. Repeated thoughts and emotional experiences influence how the brain processes future experiences. Practices such as journaling, mindfulness, and reflective awareness strengthen neural circuits associated with emotional regulation and resilience.

> *"Well-being is a skill that can be cultivated."*
> – Richard Davidson

Through intentional practices, we can strengthen the qualities that support deeper well-being.

Human Well-Being: A Simple Comparison

Happiness	Joy
Hedonic Well-being	Eudaimonic Well-being
Pleasure	Meaning
Positive Moments	Purpose
External Events	Enduring
Temporary	Connection
Celebration	Compassion
Connection	Growth

The Science of Joy and the Eight Steps of Discover the Gift

Awareness, Growth, and the Brain

The teachings of *Discover the Gift* describe a journey of awareness and transformation that many people experience as they grow through life's challenges and opportunities. While these principles arise from wisdom traditions and lived experience, modern neuroscience offers an interesting perspective on why they can be so powerful.

Research in psychology and neuroscience shows that the brain is continually adapting through a process known as neuroplasticity. Neuroplasticity refers to the brain's ability to reorganize and strengthen neural pathways in response to repeated thoughts, emotional experiences, and behaviors.

In simple terms, the way we think, reflect, and respond to our experiences gradually shapes the way the brain processes future experiences. Practices such as reflection, gratitude, compassion, and intentional awareness strengthen neural circuits associated with emotional regulation, resilience, and insight. These are the very qualities that The Eight Steps of *Discover the Gift* encourage us to cultivate. Through these steps, we learn to approach life with openness, meaning, and connection, and over time, these practices support the development of joy and well-being.

Think of a time you have experienced immense joy. Pause for a moment and go there. Be there. Feel the purity it gives you. Inhale it, hug it, and return to this moment. Joy is an embrace within which emerges and radiates throughout your being – this is why accessing it is so crucial, now more than ever. Joy reminds us of a pure state, one we can return to, which is a deep well that never runs dry, like love – it never drains and is always accessible and expansive.

Joy as an Outcome of Awareness

Joy often emerges when we live in alignment with these principles. It grows through:

- Openness to experience
- Clarity of intention
- Meaningful action
- Reflection and learning
- Emotional awareness
- Resilience through adversity
- Compassion for others
- Living from love

Through repeated practice, these qualities become more familiar. Over time, the brain begins to recognize patterns of meaning, connection, and possibility more easily. In this way, joy becomes less dependent on circumstances and more connected to awareness and understanding.

The journey of *Discover the Gift* reminds us that transformation is not about avoiding life's challenges. It is about learning to meet them with curiosity, compassion, and wisdom. Through awareness, intention, and love, we begin to recognize something profound: The experiences that once felt confusing or difficult may contain the very insights that help us grow. And as we continue to reflect, learn, and connect with others, joy begins to emerge naturally. Not as something we must search for, rather as something we discover within the meaning of our lives.

A Simple Map of Inner Transformation

The journey through The Eight Steps of Discover the Gift mirrors many of the psychological processes associated with growth and resilience. Below is a simplified way to understand how these elements interact within the brain and emotional system.

Awareness

Awareness activates the brain's reflective networks. When we pause and observe our thoughts and emotions, we engage areas of the brain associated with insight and self-understanding. Awareness is the first step toward change. And being receptive to being aware is the baseline.

Reflection

Reflection allows us to examine our experiences from a broader perspective. This process strengthens the brain's ability to integrate emotional experiences with rational understanding. Reflection often leads to insight.

Meaning

When we identify meaning in our experiences, even difficult ones, we activate psychological processes associated with resilience and post-traumatic growth. We are meaning-making machines. Use your experiences to generate new thoughts and pathways connected to your inner wisdom, your internal guidance. Meaning transforms adversity into wisdom.

Connection

Joy is strongly associated with connection, both internally and with others. Experiences of love, compassion, and belonging activate neural pathways that support emotional well-being. Connection deepens joy.

Purpose

Purpose provides direction for our actions and decisions. When we align our lives with meaningful intentions, we strengthen motivation and psychological resilience. Purpose sustains growth.

Reflection Prompt

Take a moment to pause and consider all you have just consumed:

Where in your life have you already experienced growth through awareness, reflection, connection, or purpose?

Write about a moment when something difficult eventually revealed a deeper lesson or gift.

The Science of Joy and Resilience

How Reflection, Awareness, and Writing Transform the Brain

Joy is often misunderstood as a fleeting emotion that appears only when circumstances are perfect. Yet modern psychology and neuroscience tell us something much deeper and more encouraging.

> *"Neuroscience helps us understand how the brain changes. The Discover the Gift framework offers a way to engage that change consciously, guiding awareness into alignment, where joy can emerge."*

Scientific Insights About Joy, Resilience, and the Brain

Throughout this book you will see brief insights from modern psychology and neuroscience. These are not meant to overwhelm the reflective experience. Instead, they serve as gentle reminders that the practices you are engaging in are supported by a growing body of research on human well-being.

Science continues to affirm something that many wisdom traditions have long understood: our thoughts, emotions, and attention influence the structure and function of the brain. When we cultivate awareness, compassion, gratitude, and purpose, we are strengthening neural pathways that support emotional balance and resilience.

Positive Emotions Expand Our Capacity

Psychologist Barbara Fredrickson developed the Broaden-and-Build Theory of Positive Emotions, which explains that emotions such as joy, love, and gratitude help broaden our awareness and expand our capacity for creativity, connection, and problem-solving. Over time, these expanded states help build lasting psychological resources that support resilience. In other words, moments of joy do more than feel good. They actually help us grow stronger.

The Brain Can Change Throughout Life

Neuroscientist Richard Davidson and many others have demonstrated that the brain remains capable of change throughout our lives. Practices such as mindfulness, compassion, and reflective awareness can strengthen neural circuits associated with emotional regulation and empathy. The brain's ability to reorganize and grow is known as neuroplasticity. It means that our mental and emotional patterns are not fixed. They can evolve as our awareness grows.

Meaning and Purpose Support Well-Being

Psychologist Martin Seligman, one of the founders of modern positive psychology, has shown that well-being is supported not only by pleasure, but by meaning, engagement, relationships, and contribution. This deeper form of well-being is often what people describe as joy. Joy arises when we feel connected to something meaningful and aligned with our values.

Writing Strengthens Emotional Processing

Research on expressive writing by psychologist James Pennebaker suggests that writing about firsthand experiences can improve emotional clarity, reduce stress, and support psychological integration. Writing helps organize thoughts and experiences, allowing the brain to process complex emotions and create meaning. This is one reason reflective journaling can be such a powerful tool for growth.

Writing and the Brain

Reflective writing has been shown to support both emotional health and cognitive processing. Studies in expressive writing demonstrate that when people write honestly about their experiences, they often experience improvements in mood, clarity, and resilience.

Writing helps us:

- Organize our thoughts
- Process emotional experiences
- Identify patterns in our lives
- Create meaning from our experiences

In many ways, writing acts as a bridge between the emotional centers of the brain and the regions responsible for insight and understanding.

Neuroplasticity, Well-Being, and the Emergence of Joy

Neuroscience suggests that the brain remains plastic throughout the lifespan, continually adapting in response to repeated thoughts, emotions, behaviors, and relational experiences (Doidge, 2007; Davidson & McEwen, 2012). This ongoing capacity for change, known as neuroplasticity, reflects the brain's ability to reorganize and strengthen neural pathways in response to how we engage with life.

In recent years, research has increasingly focused on emotional well-being as a measurable and biologically relevant construct. While the scientific literature more commonly examines constructs such as positive affect, eudaimonic well-being, resilience, compassion, and mindfulness rather than joy specifically, these domains provide meaningful insight into the conditions through which joy may arise (Ryan & Deci, 2001; Fredrickson, 2001; recent reviews, 2024–2025).

Emerging evidence suggests that practices such as mindfulness, reflection, compassion, gratitude, and intentional awareness influence neural systems associated with emotional regulation, attention, reward processing, and social connection. These systems are largely mediated through interactions between prefrontal regulatory networks and limbic structures involved in emotional processing (Davidson & Begley, 2012; recent neuroimaging reviews, 2024).

Mindfulness research offers one of the clearest contemporary pathways linking practice and neuroplastic change. Recent reviews report that mindfulness-based interventions are associated with measurable changes in both brain structure and function, including reduced amygdala reactivity, improved emotional regulation, and enhanced resilience to stress. While these findings do not isolate joy as a singular outcome, they support the broader conclusion that intentional inner practices can cultivate the neural conditions associated with deeper well-being (recent mindfulness review, 2024).

Resilience research further strengthens this understanding. Current models describe resilience not as a fixed trait, but as an adaptive and dynamic process involving cognitive reappraisal, emotional regulation, and neurobiological flexibility (Southwick & Charney, 2012; recent resilience frameworks, 2025). Increased engagement of the prefrontal cortex supports reflection, meaning-making, and adaptive response, while decreased reactivity in threat-related systems contributes to emotional stability.

Within this context, adversity is no longer viewed solely as a source of distress. When engaged with consciously, it can become a catalyst for integration, growth, and expanded perspective. This aligns closely with the Discover the Gift philosophy, which emphasizes awareness, reflection, and meaning as pathways to transformation.

Recent qualitative research on joy itself highlights an important distinction. While still underexplored as a discrete construct, participants consistently describe joy not as fleeting pleasure, but as something cultivated through meaning, connection, gratitude, and context (recent qualitative study, 2025). This reinforces the distinction between happiness as a momentary experience and joy as a deeper, more integrated state.

Additionally, current research on compassion and connectedness continues to demonstrate that relational experience plays a vital role in both neuroplasticity and well-being. Studies indicate that compassion-based practices and social connection are associated with measurable changes in neural systems related to empathy, trust, and emotional regulation (recent compassion and connectedness studies, 2025).

Taken together, these findings support a clear and grounded conclusion:

The brain remains plastic.
Experience shapes that plasticity.
And we have the capacity to engage in that process consciously.

From a scientific perspective, it is more accurate to say that research supports the conditions through which joy can emerge, rather than proving joy as a singular, isolated construct. Within the Discover the Gift framework, this distinction becomes meaningful.

Joy is not something that is externally acquired or dependent solely on circumstance. It is an emergent experience, one that arises as awareness deepens, resilience strengthens, and alignment is more fully lived.

Not as something we chase.
Not as something we force.
But as something that unfolds through our engagement with life.

JOY IS ALIGNMENT, LIVED.

Discover the Gift–Philosophy of Joy

Awareness, Transformation, and the Science of Human Growth

At the heart of *Discover the Gift* is a simple yet powerful understanding: every experience contains the potential for insight, growth, and transformation. Life continually offers us moments that invite awareness. Some of these moments arrive as joy and celebration. Others arrive through challenge, uncertainty, or change. Yet within every experience lies the opportunity to discover something meaningful.

Discover the Gift's philosophy: transformation begins with awareness. When we pause to observe our experiences with curiosity rather than judgment, we begin to recognize the lessons that life is offering.

Modern neuroscience supports this understanding. Research in neuroplasticity shows that the brain is continually shaped by our thoughts, attention, and emotional experiences. When we reflect on our lives with openness and intention, we strengthen neural pathways associated with resilience, emotional regulation, and insight. In other words, awareness does not simply change how we think. Awareness changes the brain.

Reflection, gratitude, compassion, and purposeful action all influence the way our minds process experience. Over time, these practices help cultivate greater clarity, adaptability, and well-being.

The Eight Steps of *Discover the Gift* offers a practical framework for engaging this process. Receptivity invites us to remain open to new perspectives. Intention helps us align our awareness with what matters most. Activation moves insight into meaningful action. Infinite Feedback reminds us that life continually offers guidance. Vibration encourages us to cultivate thoughts and emotions that elevate our inner state. Adversity and Transformation reveal the wisdom that can emerge from challenge. Creating a Conscious and Compassionate World reminds us that our choices shape humanity's collective experience. Love brings all these principles together as the foundation of connection and meaning.

Through these steps, we begin to see our experiences differently. We begin to recognize that growth is not something that happens once. It is an ongoing spiral process of awareness, reflection, and choice.

Joy emerges naturally when we live in alignment with these principles. It appears when we recognize and create meaning within our experiences. It grows when we cultivate compassion toward ourselves and others. And it deepens when we remember that every moment holds the potential for discovery.

Joy, Alignment, and the Expression of Our Gifts

Something profound begins to unfold when we live in alignment with who we truly are. Not as a concept. Not as an idea. But as a lived experience.

Modern research in psychology and neuroscience continues to point toward a powerful truth. Well-being deepens not simply through what we achieve, but through how we live in relationship with ourselves. It grows through alignment with our values, engagement with what feels meaningful, and the expression of our natural strengths.

What many studies refer to as eudaimonic well-being speaks directly to this. It is not about fleeting pleasure. It is about living with purpose, authenticity, and inner congruence. When we begin to discover our gifts and allow them to be expressed, something shifts within us, freeing us from the striving to become something we are not. We are returning to what has always been true. And from that place, joy begins to emerge.

Research on flow states offers another window into this experience. When we are fully engaged in what we love, when our abilities meet meaningful challenge, we enter a state of deep presence. Time softens. Self-doubt quiets. There is a sense of immersion that feels both effortless and expansive. These are not just moments of productivity. They are moments of alignment. And within that alignment, a deeper form of fulfillment becomes available.

> *"Joy lives there.*
> *It is not something we chase.*
> *It is something we experience when we are fully engaged in what is true."*

There is also a growing body of research showing that positive emotional states do more than feel good. They expand our awareness, increase creativity, deepen connection, and build long-term resilience. Over time, these experiences begin to reinforce themselves. As we live in alignment, we experience greater clarity. That clarity supports more aligned choices. Those choices deepen connection and meaning. And from that, a natural expansion occurs.

> *"This is where joy begins to grow.*
> *Not in a linear way.*
> *But in a way that builds, deepens, and expands over time."*

When we follow what we are naturally drawn toward, when we live from our strengths and engage in what feels meaningful, we also meet fundamental human needs. We experience a sense of autonomy, competence, and connection. These are not abstract ideas. They are foundational to our psychological well-being.

> *"Which means that living your gifts is not indulgent.*
> *It is essential."*

It supports the very systems within you that allow you to feel grounded, connected, and alive.

And as life unfolds, we begin to see something even more powerful. Joy is not dependent on life being easy. It deepens as meaning becomes clearer. Research on resilience shows that when we reflect on our experiences, especially the challenging ones, and begin to find meaning within them, our capacity for well-being expands. We become more adaptable. More aware. More connected to what truly matters.

This is the heart of transformation. Within the *Discover the Gift* framework, this is where everything comes together. We begin by becoming receptive. We clarify intention. We act. We listen through feedback. We become aware of our internal state. We grow through adversity. We deepen connection. Love shapes our lives.

Each of these steps is not separate from science. They are ways of consciously engaging the very processes that research now confirms support growth, resilience, and well-being.

> *"Neuroscience helps us understand how the brain changes. The Discover the Gift framework helps us understand how to live that change."*

And as we do, something remarkable begins to happen. Joy does not arrive as something outside of us. It emerges as we live in alignment with what is true. It grows as we express our gifts. It deepens as we engage with meaning. It expands as we connect, reflect, and evolve.

> *"Joy is living in alignment.*
> *And the more we live it, the more it grows."*

The journey of *Discover the Gift* is not about eliminating life's challenges. It is about transforming the way we meet them. Through awareness, intention, and love, we begin to recognize the deeper truth that has always been present: The gift we seek has always lived within us. The secret is that you are the gift. Your willingness to discover your authentic nature is a domino effect, like a cast stone in a still pond–the ripples continue to cultivate and create a life you love living.

How Joy Expands as We Discover Our Gifts and Follow Our Passions

There is strong research supporting the idea that joy is not random. It grows through alignment, engagement, and meaning. While science does not always use the word joy, it consistently studies closely related states such as eudaimonic well-being (meaning and purpose), flow states (deep engagement), intrinsic motivation (doing what we are naturally drawn to), and self-concordance (alignment with one's authentic self).

And across all of these, a consistent pattern emerges: when people engage in activities aligned with their strengths, values, and passions, well-being deepens and becomes more sustainable over time.

Joy Grows Through Alignment

Research in positive psychology shows that living in alignment with one's values and purpose leads to deeper and more stable well-being than pleasure alone. Carol Ryff's work on psychological well-being identifies purpose in life, personal growth, and authenticity as core drivers of lasting fulfillment. Studies show that individuals who live with purpose experience greater emotional stability, resilience, and life satisfaction.

When we discover our gifts, we are not adding something new. We are aligning with what is already true. And from that alignment, joy begins to stabilize and deepen.

JOY EXPANDS THROUGH ENGAGEMENT

Mihaly Csikszentmihalyi's research on flow shows that when people engage in activities that match their skills and stretch their abilities, they enter a state of deep focus, timelessness, and intrinsic fulfillment. This state is consistently associated with higher life satisfaction and well-being.

People report their highest levels of fulfillment not from passive pleasure but from meaningful engagement. When we live our gifts, we become absorbed in life. And in that absorption, joy is not pursued. It is experienced.

JOY BUILDS MOMENTUM

Barbara Fredrickson's Broaden-and-Build Theory shows that positive emotional states expand awareness, increase creativity, strengthen relationships, and build long-term psychological resources. Over time, this creates an upward spiral of well-being.

When someone begins to express their gifts, follow what feels meaningful, and engage with life intentionally, they experience more positive emotional states. Those states expand perception, increase opportunities, deepen connection, and reinforce aligned behavior. This creates a self-reinforcing loop.

INTRINSIC MOTIVATION AND AUTHENTIC LIVING

Edward Deci and Richard Ryan's Self-Determination Theory shows that well-being increases when three fundamental needs are met: autonomy (being true to yourself), competence (using your strengths), and relatedness (connection with others). Following your passions naturally fulfills all three.

Living your gifts is not indulgent. It is psychologically regulating and growth supportive.

Resilience and Meaning Amplify Joy Over Time

Research on resilience shows that meaning-making during challenge increases long-term well-being, and that people who integrate their experiences into purpose report greater life satisfaction and emotional strength. This aligns directly with Adversity and Transformation: joy does not grow because life becomes easier. It grows because meaning becomes clearer.

Current research in psychology and neuroscience suggests that well-being deepens when individuals live in alignment with their values, engage meaningfully with their strengths, and cultivate awareness through intentional practices. Studies on flow, intrinsic motivation, and eudaimonic well-being consistently demonstrate that fulfillment is not derived solely from external achievement, but from the experience of living in alignment with one's authentic self.

Within the *Discover the Gift* framework, this alignment is expressed through the recognition and embodiment of one's gifts. As these gifts are lived and shared, positive emotional states expand awareness, strengthen resilience, and build meaningful connections. In this way, joy does not simply appear as a momentary experience. It grows, deepens, and expands as a natural expression of alignment lived over time.

> *"Joy expands as we live our gifts,*
> *not because life becomes perfect,*
> *but because we become aligned with what is true."*

Your environment shapes nervous systems, perception, identity, behavior, and even what we believe is possible for us. Human beings are not separate from their environments. We are constantly responding to them, consciously and unconsciously.

During events like COVID-19 pandemic, many people were placed into environments that intensified stress, conflict, isolation, fear, financial strain, or emotional exhaustion. Some people were suddenly trapped in spaces that did not support their emotional or psychological well-being. And for many, there truly was no immediate choice.

What becomes important then is understanding that while we may not always control the external environment, we can begin cultivating an internal environment.

That does not mean pretending circumstances are okay when they are not. It does not mean bypassing pain. And it does not mean people should simply "think positively."

It means creating access.

Access to breath. Access to awareness. Access to meaning. Access to regulation. Access to moments of safety within the self.

Healthy growth is never separated from conditions. If a plant is wilting, we do not shame it. We examine sunlight, soil, water, temperature, space, nourishment, and care. Humans require the same compassionate lens.

The nervous system asks questions constantly: Am I safe? Am I seen? Am I trapped? Am I connected? Do I belong? Can I rest? Can I express myself honestly here?

And when the answer to those questions becomes chronically "no," the body adapts for survival rather than flourishing.

So the deeper question becomes: How do we become an environment for ourselves when the external world cannot yet fully support us?

Perhaps it begins with small acts of internal cultivation:

- Creating moments of stillness, even inside chaos
- Protecting what enters the mind and body
- Building internal language that is compassionate rather than violent
- Finding one safe person, one safe practice, one safe space
- Allowing emotion to move instead of suppressing it
- Remembering that survival responses are adaptations, not identity
- Reconnecting to meaning, creativity, beauty, nature, breath, music, prayer, movement, or purpose

Because eventually the goal is not merely survival.

It is creating enough inner stability that we can begin making different choices when choices become available.

And sometimes the first form of freedom is not changing the environment immediately. Sometimes it is recognizing: "This environment is affecting me." "This is not all that I am." "My nervous system is responding to conditions." "There is wisdom in my response." "And somewhere within me, life still wants to grow."

Just like the flower.

No mud, no lotus.

DISCOVER THE GIFT – THE EIGHT STEPS

Each of The Eight Steps can be understood as a practice that strengthens specific aspects of awareness and emotional resilience.

THE EIGHT STEPS

At the heart of this work lies a foundational understanding: the mind, emotions, and conditioning shape how people behave, what they believe, and how they perceive the world. Though deeply ingrained, these influences do not eliminate choice. Transformation begins with selfawareness and the willingness to evolve. Feeling "stuck" is often less the result of external limitation than of unconscious patterns that go unexamined. When individuals transform themselves, the effects ripple outward into families, communities, and beyond.

The human mind is designed to recognize patterns, relying on past experiences to predict and navigate the future. While this once served survival, these same mechanisms now operate beneath conscious awareness, shaping reactions in modern life. Emotions, too, play a powerful role, acting as internal messengers that point toward fulfillment and purpose. Moments of joy, engagement, and aliveness offer valuable clues to one's unique Gifts.

Yet conditioning extends beyond the personal. Cultural expectations, family histories, and inherited belief systems–religious, social, or ideological–often go unquestioned, even when they limit growth. Transformation requires interrupting these patterns and recognizing that beliefs, however deeply held, are not absolute truths but interpretations open to revision.

This inquiry leads to unity consciousness: the understanding that all beings are interconnected within a single field of energy. Every thought, word, and action carries a vibration, influencing both the individual and the collective. Like musicians in a symphony, each person contributes a distinct note, gaining power and clarity when aligned with the whole.

The Eight Steps that emerged from this realization form the framework of *Discover the Gift*:

1. Receptivity
2. Intention
3. Activation
4. Infinite Feedback
5. Vibration
6. Adversity and Transformation
7. Creating a Conscious and Compassionate World
8. Love: The Ultimate Gift

Together, these steps encompass the emotional and spiritual

spectrum of human experience. Though presented linearly, they are interdependent and continuously interacting, much like light refracted through a prism. Each appears distinct, yet all arise from, and return to, a single source.

As these principles are integrated into daily life, old patterns begin to loosen their grip. Energy increases, awareness deepens, and a sense of balance emerges. This state, described as being "present to one's own presence," allows for greater ease and flexibility, making it possible to navigate life with clarity rather than struggle, and with compassion rather than selfjudgment.

Each person is a unique expression of universal energy, as distinct as a fingerprint or snowflake. By embracing this individuality and consciously choosing new pathways, authentic power is revealed. And through that commitment, transformation becomes not only possible, but inevitable.

Each step is accompanied by a mandala and offered as a tool for reflection and meditation. These visual forms serve as a direct pathway to inner awareness. As His Holiness the Dalai Lama notes, mandalas have a unique capacity to engage the mind, using visual imagery to convey deep feeling, insight, and values such as compassion and forgiveness.

When all of these centers are in balance, they form what is described as the Unified Field of Love, where all mandalas and chakras converge. In this alignment, harmony is restored, and love is experienced as a natural state of being.

As you move through The Eight Steps of *Discover the Gift*, increasing awareness supports the gradual opening and integration of the philosophy of this process.

– Shajen Joy Aziz, M.Ed., M.A.

Step One: Receptivity

The Moment Everything Begins

> *"Receptivity invites openness. When we remain receptive to new perspectives and experiences, we activate the brain's reflective networks and increase our ability to see possibilities that might otherwise remain hidden. Openness creates the foundation for learning and growth."*

Transformation begins the moment you stop running. Not physically. Internally.

Receptivity is the willingness to pause long enough to see what is actually here. Not what you hoped would be here. Not what you've been telling yourself is here. But what is real, present, and alive within you?

This is not passive. It is one of the most courageous acts you will ever take. Because the moment you become receptive, you begin to notice what has been waiting for your attention. The emotions you have bypassed. The thoughts you have avoided. The patterns you have repeated without fully seeing. And yet, this is where everything begins.

Modern neuroscience confirms that awareness itself activates regulatory brain systems, particularly within the prefrontal cortex, interrupting automatic behavioral loops and allowing new neural pathways to form (Tang et al., 2017). Without awareness, the brain defaults to efficiency, repeating what is familiar. With awareness, it becomes adaptive. Receptivity is the doorway into that awareness.

There is a quiet power in allowing yourself to see clearly. It removes illusion. It dissolves distortion. It brings you into a direct relationship with your life. And in that relationship, something shifts.

You are no longer reacting unconsciously. You are present. And presence changes everything. Receptivity invites a different question: What is here that I have not yet allowed myself to see? Not to fix it. Not to change it immediately. But to acknowledge it.

Acknowledge. Not conceptually. But honestly.
Because what you do not acknowledge… You cannot transform.

Meditation: Opening to the Life That Is Here

Close your eyes for a moment.
And just breathe.

Slowly breathing in.
And gently breathing out.

And perhaps for this moment, you do not need to rush anywhere. You do not need to solve everything. You do not need to hold the weight of the entire world all at once.

Simply arrive here.

Notice your breath.
Notice your body.
Notice the thoughts moving through your awareness without needing to chase them or push them away.

Just notice.

You see, so many of us learned to move through life bracing ourselves. Preparing. Protecting. Anticipating what could go wrong. And over time, what begins to happen is that the nervous system becomes accustomed to survival. We stay alert, but disconnected. Functioning, but not fully present.

And yet presence changes things.

The moment we slow down enough to become aware, something within us begins softening.

Receptivity is not weakness. In many ways, it is courage. It is the willingness to remain open to life even after disappointment. Even after uncertainty. Even after moments that hardened parts of us we once believed would always remain soft.

And flexibility is wisdom.

Nature reminds us of this constantly. The tree that bends survives the storm. Water adapts to every environment it enters, and still remains fully itself.

There is something deeply meaningful about that.

You are allowed to evolve.
You are allowed to outgrow old stories.
You are allowed to become someone your younger self could not yet imagine.

And perhaps healing begins there.
Not in forcing ourselves to change, but in finally allowing ourselves to become.

Take another breath.

The body listens.
The nervous system responds.
Awareness changes the experience itself.

Quietly repeat within yourself:

"I am open to this moment."
"I allow myself to grow and adapt."
"I release the need to control everything."
"I trust myself to meet life as it unfolds."

And for just a moment longer, breathe.

Because perhaps receptivity begins the moment we stop resisting our own lives.

"Research in mindfulness and emotional regulation continues to affirm what many wisdom traditions have always known: when we consciously slow the breath and bring awareness into the present moment, the body begins shifting out of stress reactivity and into greater balance and coherence."

"We incarnate to release the Gifts, the talents, the passages and the powers that are within us…We are really God's Gift to the world. We are the Universe becoming fully conscious of itself, in fully giving of ourselves to this world."

– **Dr. Michael Bernard Beckwith**

Minister, Author, Humanitarian, Musician
Founder & Spiritual Director, Agape International Spiritual Center

Pillars of Joy

by Cindy Davis

Joy is found in the whole of who I am. Embracing each part of my existence. Embracing my femininity and stepping into the power and strength I was afraid of experiencing…my sensuality.

I am Cindy Davis.

Until my divorce at 40, I lived by a definition of "Good Girl" that I understood to mean: be polite, stay covered up, be modest and find your one true love who will sweep you off your feet and you'll live happily ever after. While this message made sense on some level, inside there was a fire that couldn't be extinguished, and it terrified me. It did not feel like it fit the definition I was supposed to live by, so I stuffed it down. I got married in my early 20s and while I thought marriage meant I was finally growing up and could sit at the adult table, I soon realized there was only shame and judgment to be found, and no room for growth, safety or exploration.

I kept up the "Good Girl" façade, keeping my fire suppressed, because that was the expectation. And there was so much fear. Fear of myself, fear of disappointing others, fear of judgment & shame, fear of this growing fire inside that never went away. I didn't feel worthy of myself, so I held back and made sure others lived. I spent years doing what was expected of me, because that was safe and what "Good Girls" do; when all the while, I was slowly dying inside. I sacrificed myself and my joy for the joy of others, losing myself while trying to create happiness and ease for others. In the midst of life, I forgot that *my* joy was actually the most important.

As part of my decision to divorce, I decided it was time to step away from the image of "Good Girl" that I previously understood, and step into curiosity. I wanted to learn about this growing fire inside me and who I was with it. I went from turtlenecks and high neck blouses to fitted camisoles and deep necklines, from trouser socks and loafers to fishnets and heels. It was liberating and I felt

alive. I loved feeling my skirts swish around my legs and hearing my heels click on the floor as I walked down the hall. For the first time ever, I felt beautiful, magnetic, sensual, and oh-so-feminine.

For a year, I explored my mind and heart, said yes to things I wanted to do and found curiosity in, and questioned a lot of life rules I had lived by. I redefined "Good Girl" to encompass a foundation of pillars, ways of living that had always been a part of me, while also finally acknowledging this fire inside, owning where my joy and life source stems from... my sacred, feminine sensuality.

Making the decision to live from a place of sensuality changed my view of the world in the most beautiful ways. While my sensuality was in part about sex and that amazing world, I also felt joy and life in ways I had never experienced before. All the pillars I lived from began to feel stronger and more solid. I walked taller, I spoke louder and without hesitation. I stood grounded when I needed to, and making hard decisions became easier. My entire existence was aflame because I was finally listening to myself and what was necessary for me to live completely.

For the first time in my life, "Good Girl" meant freedom, and my Pillars of Joy cleared the way for more than I could have imagined. I began to realize that owning my sacred femininity meant every other aspect of my life was able to become grounded and centered. I was no longer holding back this primal instinct to feel whole and stand confidently as the amazing woman I was becoming. I was challenging the fears I'd placed on myself and let myself submit to a life of joy. There was still a lot of learning to do. New questions about myself and what I wanted from life emerged, including what future relationships may look like. I had opened a door I was never going to close again, so to honor myself and the work that had been done, it was imperative to have a clear understanding of what I had to offer and what I wanted from another.

I am now over 10 years into this discovery of Joy, and it has been an amazing and, at times, difficult journey. Owning my sensuality is sacred; it is feminine, it is passionate, and it is powerful! Living from this core is for those ready to stand strong on a foundation of vulnerability, love, magic, connection, and spirituality.

Here is what I gained through discovering my Gift of Joy:

- I became grounded in Passion
    - Passion for Life

- Passion for Love
- Passion for Joy

- I became my own creator of magic, finally giving myself that wonder and awe I'd freely given to others
- I became an advocate for my own needs and connected with others who aligned with my journey
- I became a guide of energy and light for other women to recognize in themselves
- I became the Good Girl I always knew I was…a woman who owns her sacred sensuality and creates joy from its fire of life

I'm in love with the beauty of who I am as a woman, a soul, a lover and my Gifts are worthy of being shared with the world. I am magic and magnificent, innocent, and vulnerable. I am strength and knowledge and love, and an unwavering powerhouse of Joy.

My Pillars of Joy:

1. **Love.** This is my source of compassion and empathy, love of self, love of life and living, love for others. This is where integrity and boundaries are cherished and held sacred.
2. **Magic.** This is my source of imagination and awe, where the childlike wonder of life explores the lands of castles and dragons and sees the ethereal elves with the naked eye.
3. **Connection.** This is my source of relationships with others and holding sacred those who are worthy of my energy.
4. **Spirituality.** This is my source of embodying the energy of myself, my sisters and all my foremothers. Honoring their

strength, knowledge, love, and their hurt, while remaining connected with Earth, Nature, and channeling the elements in every moment of every day.

5. **Sensuality.** My source of Sacred Femininity. Where my passion for living, loving, magic, connection and spirituality find their heart. This is my source of joy, pleasure, passion, fun, and desire for success. This is my source of power and strength, where my vulnerability turns into courage, and my fears are given the doorway to walk through and experience the gifts on the other side.

❋❋❋

CINDY DAVIS is a Certified Passion Test Facilitator, Author of *Discover the Gift of Joy: How to Experience Joy in Life, Work and Relationships* and Life Coach for women ready to shed their old definitions of Good Girl and embrace their powerhouse of Joy through their sacred feminine sensuality.

cindy@burningembersllc.com
burningembersllc.wordpress.com
@coachcidfirewithin

Survival to Sovereignty

by Katie Albee

> *"The privilege of a lifetime is to become who you truly are."*
> - Carl Jung

My colorfully chaotic childhood led me on the path of discovering true healing from the inside out at a very young age. I found the more I tried to live within society's terms, the more unfulfilled, unhappy, and unhealthy I became. Over time, I learned to trust my intuition and live authentically and unapologetically.

In the past decade, I have journeyed deeply into healing, quantum science, and personal development to find the gift of joy in life. Through my own healing, I uncovered the holistic connection between the mental, physical, emotional, and spiritual realms. In this journey, I have become the gift, embodying conscious choice -serving my clients as a catalyst for change through the way I live, heal, and listen within.

Our first house fire happened when I was 4 years old. In that memory, I am standing at the stairs as a man burst through our front door yelling, "Your f*@#ing house is on fire!" I look toward the couch and see myself sitting there with my 14-year-old brother. In the next moment, I am back in my body, looking up the stairs at the fire and the firemen with awe and wonderment. That day left two deep imprints: dissociation, and fear intertwined with excitement. Years later, I understood that this moment shaped how I perceived the world and learned to be able to stand both inside an experience and witness it from the outside. What once protected me eventually became my doorway into conscious choice.

My Head Start teacher once told my mom that I had "unique abilities" that the other kids did not express. Being named as different, paired with the spiritual intensity of the fire, taught me to hide my gifts and dissociate from them.

I grew up in Utah, spiritual, not religious. On my 6th birthday, a little girl left my party in tears because we did not have any pictures of Jesus on the walls. This moment led me to ask the question, "Who created God?" When no one could answer this, I began to dissociate from God.

At age 8, we had another house fire. After that, I began to believe that at age 12, we would have to move again because of flames; however, this time it was a fire within my mom. One day she decided that she was going to pack up and move to the canyon. I wrote her a letter expressing my fears; she read the letter and simply crumpled it up and dropped it on the ground. I did not realize what was going on within her or within me. I did know that she no longer had the capacity to take care of me, and that I would have to learn how to navigate this big world on my own.

My mom was a hippie, deeply connected to the Earth; she

instilled this within us. We went to powwows and we had different spiritual practices, strengthening our connection with Mama Gaia and all her inhabitants. So even though I felt alone, I knew that I was supported, protected, and relatively safe.

I moved between homes several times, teaching me adaptability, resilience, to read the energy of the room, and how to fit in just enough to stay safe. At 11 years old, I had a strong inner calling to move West, toward the ocean, toward new possibilities. I didn't yet have the language for intuition. As soon as I graduated, I took the leap and moved to Oregon. I had no concrete plans; I moved from instinct rather than logic, guided by an inner calling to seek joy. I tried several different practical jobs, yet none of them fulfilled me. I sensed there was something more, a deep inner calling to unfold even more of my gifts to share with the world.

At age 15, I began my own tie-dye business. As the youngest of four, I simply wanted to make some cash. Now, at age 42, I realize life is cyclical and happening *for* us rather than *to* us. This creative art helped me ground, heal my chakras, and create a sense of safety for myself, long before I understood the deeper impact of color and art as medicine for myself and others.

Over the years of pursuing joy, my life has taken many turns and many paths, ultimately teaching me that true joy lives in this present moment. In my pursuit, I studied trauma, Reiki, Theta Healing, and countless modalities, always coming back to the same truth: when we bring our energy back to our inner world, our outer life naturally reorganizes.

Our nervous systems were not designed to live in a world where we are governed by chaos, fear, and constant proving. When the system becomes overwhelmed, it may dissociate, not as a failure, but as a protective response, a way the body keeps us safe when it doesn't feel possible to stay present.

When we learn to regulate our nervous system, we regain access to our inner world. We begin to feel our feelings, learn to be comfortable being uncomfortable, to question conditioning, and to listen to the wisdom of the body. From this place, we no longer abandon ourselves. We listen. We feel. We remember.

Let's reconnect together. Place your feet on the earth, outside, if possible, inside if needed. Allow your breath to drop into your belly and imagine the ground holding you the way loving ancestors would. Place one hand on your heart and the other on your lower belly. As you inhale, feel your spine lengthen, breathing all the way to its base. As you exhale, sense your body gently lighten up from the root as your awareness rises to your third eye. Continue this steady rhythm, allowing each breath to soften the heart from within. Notice what shifts when you remember you are supported.

And with that, we know that joy is no longer something we search for, yet a way of being that we allow. Presence becomes a portal, and every moment becomes a gift. Every event carries a treasure, even if it doesn't feel like it. These "challenges" are shaping and redirecting us.

Reflect on a "challenge" in your life that later revealed itself as a gift.

What did this experience give me that I couldn't have received any other way?

If this moment was working for me rather than against me, what might it have been teaching me about who I'm becoming?

You can find recorded reflections for both practices on my website, where I explore this reframe more deeply.

I invite you to create an altar to honor your inner child. A space of memory and safety where younger parts are welcomed home, fragmentation softens, and the soul remembers its innate wholeness through presence, compassion, and conscious choice.

❋❋❋

Katie Albee

Soul Midwife: Regulating Your Nervous System, Reconnecting with Your Soul

801-228-7923
www.root-awakening.com
Facebook: Katie Albee
YouTube: @RootAwakeningKatieAlbee

Powered by Kindness: Experience the Authentic Joy

by Maria Luisa M. Carter (Lulu)

Deep Sense of Appreciation

First, I am very grateful to you for reading this chapter. My name is Maria Luisa, but you can call me Lulu. I am originally from Brazil. I am a diligent worker and a person committed to my purpose. I believe in the extraordinary work of service to others. When I decided to write this chapter, I opened myself to my intuition and decided to write about my journey to Joy in Haiti. And I would like to invite you to reflect on your journey to joy as you read this chapter.

Since the COVID-19 pandemic, I have developed a greater sense of gratitude for being in nature. I became an observer, a cheerleader, and a passionate person who adores plants, flowers, butterflies, and bees. The dragonflies dancing around my garden, my sanctuary, remind me of the delicate beauty of this world.

However, I often find myself contemplating the contrast between two realities that coexist within each of us: one that inflicts pain, sorrow, sadness, and perhaps a feeling of helplessness, and another that opens our hearts to joy, peace, and hope for our future.

A Perspective of Joy

Joy, I've come to see, isn't dependent on external circumstances. It begins from within, nourished by kindness, gratitude, and empathy.

It's the quiet force that reminds us that we are not isolated but rather are interconnected in a web of life shared by humanity.

A simple smile, brief eye contact, a warm word – all these small acts carry the seeds of joy. Authenticity in kindness sparks a luminous feeling that can change both the giver and the receiver. When we extend compassion, be it through a gentle touch, a listening ear, or a moment of silent understanding, we plant a seed. And that seed has the potential to grow into a radiant flower of hope that blooms even in the darkest moments.

In life's most difficult moments of suffering and grief, kindness becomes an act of radical resilience. When a friend is weighed down by sorrow, a kind gesture–offering comfort, holding a hand, sharing silence - becomes a lifeline. Such acts don't erase pain but help us navigate through it, transforming sorrow into a shared human experience of healing.

Reflecting on My Life's Lesson

Haiti became my biggest lesson, when I accepted an invitation to volunteer on January 12, 2010, just after the devastating earthquake that struck the nation. The decision was filled with uncertainty and fear; I wrestled with questions about safety, access to clean water, and the availability of food. Despite these challenges, my heart urged me to say "yes." This decision marked the beginning of an eye-opening journey that transcended any conventional form of education I had previously experienced. It was an opportunity to immerse myself in a culture facing unprecedented hardship, while providing support to those in desperate need.

Upon arriving in Haiti, I was confronted by a reality that was difficult to face. I witnessed the remnants of homes and hospitals reduced to rubble. The sight of people covered in blood and mud, and resorting to eating dirt to minimize their hunger, was heart-wrenching. This profound devastation was not just a backdrop; it was a reminder of the fragility of life and the resilience of the human spirit in the face of unimaginable adversity. I quickly realized that this experience was unlike anything I had learned in textbooks or classrooms. It taught me the importance of deep empathy, connection, and understanding in a world that often emphasizes materialistic things, superficial relationships, and division.

Serving in such a desperate environment offered unparalleled lessons in resilience. I learned how to communicate effectively in the face of adversity, often relying on non-verbal cues and shared human experiences to bridge language barriers. The people of Haiti demonstrated an extraordinary capacity for hope and determination, inspiring me to cultivate my own resilience. Their strength and unity in the face of catastrophe served as deep lessons about the power of community and the ability to rise from the ashes. Ultimately, my time in Haiti transformed my perspective on life, teaching me that the most significant lessons often come from the experiences that challenge us the most.

Witnessing the same Haitian church transform over the

years into a hospital, and then evolve into a place of healing, faith, and ultimate joy, was a profound experience for me. Returning year after year proved to be the best decision of my life, as I observed the incredible metamorphosis from pain to joy within the community.

The vibrant church life, especially among the children, was a testament to resilience and hope, while the returning missionaries infused love and support, positioning it at the center of their universe. This journey not only enriched my understanding of the human spirit but also deepened my appreciation for the transformative power of faith and community.

Transcending Moment

My ten years of volunteering in Haiti revealed to me that, even in chaos, poverty, and hardship, joy can blossom into something miraculous, an unexpected light that touches everything. It was in those moments, surrounded by the raw energy of life and suffering, that I finally understood the profound interconnection between kindness and joy: that acts of genuine compassion have the power to ignite hope and transform despair into beauty.

The Blend of Kindness and Joy

When we choose to extend empathy and show care, we craft a ripple effect that reverberates outward, touching lives in ways we may never fully realize.

Together, kindness and joy sustain us, reminding us that happiness isn't about external pleasures or perfect circumstances, but about how generously we open our hearts to others.

It's like the everyday pairing of bread and butter: simple, essential, nourishing.

Joy rooted in kindness isn't just a feeling, but a conscious choice, a way of seeing life through a prism of compassion and hope.

Whether it's a smile in moments of solitude, comfort in times of pain, or an act of love in everyday life, each gesture amplifies the unseen, unbreakable thread connecting us all. Like the shimmering leaves in my garden or the soft caress of wind, these moments teach us that genuine joy is found in a genuine connection.

It's in recognizing that, regardless of external circumstances, we possess an innate capacity to bring light into the world through acts of kindness. And in doing so, we realize that happiness isn't something we chase but something we cultivate within ourselves and in others.

"In a world often overwhelmed by suffering and chaos, kindness and joy are acts of rebellion, powerful declarations that life is precious and love is eternal.

They are the silent warriors who help us transform despair into hope and grief into grace.

It is in simple gestures, genuine care, and sincere gratitude that we discover the true magic of joy. It is a gift that we carry within, waiting to be shared, each act creating a spark that can ignite the collective spirit, making the world a little brighter, a little gentler."

LULU CARTER

To learn more, **visit www.poweredbykindness.org**

Step Two: Intention

Choosing How You Live

> *"Intention directs attention and energy. Neuroscience shows that attention plays a vital role in shaping neural pathways. When we intentionally focus on meaningful goals and values, we strengthen brain patterns that support motivation and clarity. Intentional awareness helps align our thoughts and actions."*

Once you see clearly, you are invited into choice.

Intention is the moment you decide how you will meet your life. Not based on conditioning. Not based on expectation. But based on truth. Intention is not about controlling outcomes. It is about aligning your energy, attention, and behavior with what matters most.

Research shows that attention shapes neural processing. What you consistently focus on strengthens neural pathways and influences perception (Tang et al., 2017). This means intention is not abstract. It is neurological. It directs your brain. And your brain directs your experience.

Intention requires honesty. Because once you see what is true, you can no longer unknow it. And that means something must shift. This is where you recognize and know.

You recognize what is true.
You know what you are aligned with.
And from that knowing… You choose.

Meditation: Choosing the Direction of Your Life

Place your hand gently over your heart.

Take a slow breath in.
And softly exhale.

There is extraordinary power in intention.

Not pressure.
Not perfection.
Not constantly trying to prove your worth.

Intention is different.

Intention is awareness brought into motion.

It is the conscious decision to choose how you want to live. How you want to love. How you want to speak to yourself and others. How you want to move through this world while you are here.

Because the truth is, many people are not truly living consciously. They are reacting from old conditioning, old fears, old wounds, old beliefs about who they had to become in order to survive.

And yet awareness changes things.

The moment we become conscious, new possibilities begin emerging.

So gently ask yourself:

Who am I becoming?

Not who fear shaped you into.
Not who pain convinced you to become.
But who are you beneath all of that?

And perhaps the answer does not arrive all at once.

Sometimes clarity unfolds slowly. Quietly. Moment by moment as we begin listening more deeply to ourselves again.

Imagine a soft light illuminating only the next step ahead.

That is enough.

You do not need the entire path revealed before you begin walking it.

Life rarely works that way.

Research in neuroplasticity continues to show that repeated thoughts, emotional patterns, and conscious behaviors strengthen neural pathways over time. What we practice repeatedly becomes more familiar to both the brain and the body.

Which means intention matters.

Attention matters.
Language matters.
The way we speak to ourselves matters.

In many ways, intention becomes both biological and spiritual.

Quietly repeat:

"My intention guides my life."
"I choose awareness over autopilot."
"I trust the wisdom within me."
"I move forward with presence and purpose."

Take another breath.

And allow your intention to become something you embody, not merely something you wish for.

> *"I really want to be just a simple Buddhist monk, that's my selfish motivation; then, I'd get genuine freedom! (He smiles). I don't want to have this different title."*

His Holiness The Dalai Lama

The Art of Reclaiming a Joyful Life

by Analesa Berg

> *"When did you stop dancing, singing, being enchanted by stories, or comforted by the sweet territory of silence? This is where you lost your soul and how you can recover it."*
> – Angeles Arrien

My name is Analesa Berg.

After years of hiding, I am happy to say I am a transformational artist, singer, author and speaker, passionate about helping us reach our potential and come together, beyond differences, to create a more peaceful world. This is important because, like many of us, my life was not always peaceful.

My mother was movie-star gorgeous, the belle of the ball, like *Gone with the Wind*'s Scarlett O'Hara. She was radiant, and in her element, when she painted, sang, and acted on stage. But she shut that down by the time I was five years old.

I vowed not to be like mom, but you know, that rarely works. I married my very first boyfriend, straight out of college. Mom loved my beau, but she took me aside at my engagement party and said, "If you don't want to lose yourself, don't get married." She knew about that.

He was kind and said he loved me. My parents mostly criticized me. Her caring remark was out of character, so her warning didn't land. In college, I was a Voice major, singing on stage and selling my artwork. Immediately upon marrying, I stopped singing, dancing, painting and performing - all the things that brought me joy–to be the best wife and mom I could be.

Despite my storybook marriage of beautiful homes, travel, and fancy restaurants, I was shrinking on the inside, like my mother's shrinking on the outside, her body curling with scoliosis under what I suspect was the weight of unexpressed pain.

After my children were grown, I could no longer contain my craving for self-expression and expansive spiritual perspectives.

On a crisp, fall day in 1999, I entered the Omega Institute in upstate New York, to attend my first week-long seminar towards a Master's degree in Transpersonal Psychology and Healing Arts. Omega boasted winding paths, quaint cabins, nourishing food, little buddhas, gardens, and flowers everywhere. I wrote in my journal:

For eleven minutes, we closed our eyes and danced in silence, witnessed by a partner, paying close attention only to our inner experience. In my mind, I saw flames surrounding me with energy. My body moved with devotion and exuberance between the earth and the sky. I felt engulfed in a comforting, powerful force. One with my Essence, a feminine energy I had not known before. My Wild Woman Within.

I had no awareness of how stifled I had become or how far I had strayed from my core. Dancing, my mind relaxed. The protective armor I had built since childhood melted. I experienced joy, freedom, and an exhilarating sense of expansion.

Disciplines we learned, like shamanic journeying, an indigenous practice where you travel in your mind's eye to other dimensions, challenged the belief system of this nice Jewish girl who played by the rules!

I was scared sometimes. But once I let go and allowed myself to loosen the tight grip I had on reality, my perspectives expanded. Angeles Arrien, my favorite teacher, was a cultural anthropologist and master storyteller. Angeles said the ancestors look down on us and whisper, "Maybe this one will be the one to break family patterns. Maybe this one."

It became my mission to break family patterns of hiding my truth and passions to keep the peace. I reclaimed what brought me joy–painting, singing, dancing, and being on stage.

One morning in 2007, the phone rang. "Your mother... she killed herself," my Uncle Marty said from outside my mother's home, his voice shaking. "I am so sorry. The police are here now. Can you come?"

After the shock, I gathered my senses and headed to New Jersey to be with family at this heart-wrenching time.

My father had died five months before this fateful day. Cancer. She panicked. Pills. A plastic bag over her head. "Suffocation," the death certificate read. When I saw that, I nearly fainted. I knew she was unhappy. I suggested she take up painting again, but she said no. Facing the world alone was unbearable for her.

"We are going to see this with as much love as possible," I told my family as we gathered in her home that February evening. "She did the best she could." And so did we.

My mother had lost herself in her marriage. I couldn't do the same. I had to break the pattern!

Once the estate was settled, I threw myself back into my career. I traveled the world, studying what makes people tick, how to heal, reveal our highest potential, and surrender to a force of love that supports us. I spoke at conferences, led conscious leadership retreats, sang, and created inspirational artwork. I was happy.

My new, more confident, expansive way of being caused friction in my marriage. Our relationship became estranged.

"Do what you want with all this spirituality and evolutionary stuff, just know the boys and I won't be with you," he declared one day.

"I've spent years devoted to raising our boys. And now, you are threatening to separate them from me?" I thought silently, unable to respond. Finally, after decades of putting myself aside to make this marriage work, I said, "I want a divorce."

I moved north of Boston, the ocean in my backyard. Not knowing what to do, I stood in the water, waves splashing. I surrendered, "What's next?"

I heard in my ear, "You'll go to the Hebrew Texts and paint."

"What? You must be kidding! I don't write Hebrew."

"You'll go to the Hebrew Texts and paint," the deep voice in my ear insisted.

Arghhhh!

Hearing a voice in my ear was new to me, but with all that shamanic journeying, I reluctantly learned to trust unexpected guidance.

"Take 21 days, get all your food, don't talk to anyone. Put your Hebrew books and paints around you and see what happens."

"I can't take 21 days and not talk to anyone!" But eventually, I did.

I prayed to my grandpa, a misunderstood mystic in his time. "Grandpa, if I do this, please help me. I have no idea what to do!" I stocked my fridge with healthy veggies, pomegranates, dates, almonds, and cheese. I told friends and family, "I am going into silent retreat. I won't speak to you or email until I am finished. Talk to you on the other side!"

I spent 30 days in silence, more than originally instructed. I had fun! I painted my version of Hebrew letters in mandala form, combined with images from many traditions–Hindu, Christian, Muslim, ancient Egyptian, Buddhist, and Native American, because we are all One.

I am grateful I said yes to that voice and the sweet territory of silence that followed, as the 23 multi-dimensional symbols I received, "The Alphabet of Vibration," brought me back to myself and continue to reveal hidden truths I am passionate about sharing.

When did you stop singing, painting, or enjoying silence? Are you ready to reclaim your soul and unique voice?

Be courageous. Return to what brings you joy. Reach out. You are not alone.

❋❋❋

ANALESA BERG

Joyful-light.community
analesa@joyful-light.community
analesa.substack.com
Instagram: analesa.berg
Facebook: analesab
Linkedin: analesaberg

The Physiology of Joy

by Liz Rosado-McGrath, MEd

> *"Perhaps sometimes reminding ourselves that we do have a choice makes it easier to pick the harder one."*
> – Eva Melusine Thieme

By the time I turned 32, I had found my career, got married, bought a house, and become the mother I knew I had wanted to be since I was 12 years old. And in that same breath, my world was shattering into a million tiny pieces. I loved my daughter and son more than life itself, but my marriage to their truly kind but alcoholic father had become unsustainable for me. One afternoon, I was doing the usual and hiding from the inevitable. I sat down on the bed with tears dripping down my cheeks and leveling with God. Like Elijah sitting underneath the broom tree, I let God know that I intended to fall asleep and not wake up, because the pain from my perceived failures and what lay before me was too difficult and too scary to face. When I woke up, still in the same bed with dried tears, I was angry and felt very alone. But I picked myself up, and over time, put one heavy foot in front of the other. Eventually, I came to see and feel this event for the powerful moment it was.

Throughout the course of my life, I have never been one who trafficked in negativity for very long. But that mental outlook was tested many times as I began my journey forward…and more importantly, inward. I embarked on a path to return to happiness and joy, because I was exhausted from the feeling of grief in my body. I knew I was incapable of living the rest of my days in that state, but what do people do to feel better when their external circumstances are not what they desire?

My road became paved with books and people who turned into my mirrors. I reactivated my curiosity button and discovered information about the emotional guidance scale. I learned about how it worked, with its combined practices for moving toward better feelings. Lo and behold, joy sits at the top of that scale. While I discovered this approach worked seasonally, I found it to be too transitory. I was able to touch joy, but it would come and go. I wanted to wake up in the morning and *be* joyful. I wanted to hold joy in my body as a touchstone throughout my day. Surely, that is possible!

Ask and you shall receive is still true. I found my way to a teaching certification program in Mindfulness and Meditation. One of my biggest takeaways from my studies and practices is the concept of *choosing* to be in the present with greater frequency. And the real catalyst to being present and inviting joy in is to do it *without judgment*. Once I learned these things, I found my life to be calmer, freer, with an openness that

I couldn't remember experiencing before. I noticed and became aware that I was coming from a place of response rather than reacting. In fact, many of the things, people, and events that had triggered me previously were fading away. I could sit in and sit with my joy more often. I found that as I aligned with my truth, my nervous system became better regulated. I managed stress better, and I had the ability to restore my energy following a hardship more quickly. Indeed, sourcing my joy was becoming that touchstone I could return to, again and again.

One caveat is that we do not seek joy to escape life. We seek joy to experience life more fully. This is not an achievement, but its own practice. Here is an example of a daily practice where we can choose to partner with it:

1. **Arrive in your body.**
   Sit comfortably with your feet on the floor. Take three slow breaths, a bit longer on the exhale. Silently say, "I am here." This lets your nervous system know there is no emergency.

2. **Open your senses.**
   Slowly notice something you can see or hear that is pleasing or interesting, or it can be a physical sensation that feels neutral or good.

3. **Follow the Aliveness.**
   Where does life feel more awake right now? The hands? The chest?

4. **Name Without Clinging.**
   What am I feeling – ease, softness, curiosity?

5. **Offer Appreciation.**
   Give thanks for this moment; life sees you. Joy deepens when it is witnessed, not demanded.

6. **Integrate into the day.**
   Slow your walk, take a breath. Tiny choices train the body

to trust joy. Joy is patient and accompanies me when I consciously *choose* it.

I only need to *choose* it.

❋❋❋

LIZ ROSADO-MCGRATH, MED

lizmsp@yahoo.com
281-507-0049

Step Three: Activation

Living What You Know

> *"Activation moves insight into action. Taking meaningful action reinforces neural pathways associated with confidence, learning, and progress. Each action strengthens the brain's belief that growth is possible. Action transforms awareness into lived experience."*

Awareness without action remains potential.

Activation is where truth becomes lived. Not forced. But embodied. Research on flow states shows that aligned action increases engagement, clarity, and fulfillment (Nakamura & Csikszentmihalyi, 2017). When you act in alignment, something shifts internally. You begin to trust yourself. Because you are no longer thinking about who you are becoming. You are living it.

Activation does not require perfection. It requires willingness. One step. Then another. And over time, those steps become identity.

Meditation: Remembering the Gift Within You

Close your eyes.
And breathe slowly.

There is something within you that has always been there.

A presence.
A light.
A way of being that is uniquely yours.

And somewhere along the way, many of us learned to disconnect from that part of ourselves. We learned to question our worth. To compare ourselves to others. To minimize who we are in order to belong.

And yet beneath all of that conditioning, your gift remained intact.

Quietly waiting for you to remember.

Take a slow breath in and imagine a warm light glowing softly within the center of your chest.

With every breath, it expands.

Not forced.
Not performative.
Simply natural.

Because your gift is not about becoming more important than anyone else. It is about becoming more fully yourself.

Sometimes your gift is your voice.
Sometimes it is your compassion.
Your creativity.
Your resilience.
Your ability to truly listen.
Your willingness to remain open-hearted after pain.

And often we do not even realize how deeply our presence affects another human being.

A sentence can change someone.
A smile can change someone.
Being truly seen can change someone.

We affect one another constantly.

Human beings are emotional, relational, meaning-making beings. The nervous system responds to connection, safety, kindness, and belonging in profound ways. Research continues to affirm what many of us have felt intuitively all along: we heal in environments where we feel seen, safe, connected, and valued.

Activation begins the moment you stop abandoning yourself.

The moment you stop waiting for permission to fully exist as you are.

Because the truth is, you were never meant to spend your life hiding your light in order to make others comfortable.

Take another breath.

And quietly repeat:

"I honor the gift within me."
"I allow myself to be fully seen."
"My voice matters."
"My presence creates impact."

And perhaps for this moment, allow yourself to believe that fully.

"Activation necessitates focus and clarity. As my mother said when she began to teach me photography, "You should be clear about your intention. What do you want to say with that picture? What are you focusing on?" Focus is the critical issue in dealing with pictures, and it's interesting how easily that concept crosses over into everyday life. That which you focus on increases; that which you focus on brings clarity; that which gets your attention becomes manifest through your actions."

DEMIAN LICHTENSTEIN

FILMMAKER, AUTHOR

Finding My Gift

by Roy Smoothe

Discovering My Gift Through Sound, Strategy, and Shared Thought

I did not wake up one morning knowing I had a gift called Brand-Storming. I did not set out to invent a method or coin a term. What I discovered happened gradually, through movement, curiosity, and a refusal to accept the narrow lanes that creativity is often placed in.

My gift revealed itself at the intersection of three forces that shaped my life: strategic thinking, collective intelligence, and music.

For many years, these lived side by side. I worked with brands, speakers, authors, and business leaders to clarify their message and direction. I facilitated conversations where ideas sharpened through dialogue rather than presentation. And I lived inside music, not as background noise, but as a language that moves people at a level words alone rarely reach.

The breakthrough came when I stopped treating these as separate talents and allowed them to collide.

Discovering the Gift

The first time I saw a client hear their own words sung back to them, I understood what the gift was.

They did not just hear a song. They heard themselves more clearly.

Putting speeches to music is not about performance. It is about amplification. It allows a message to travel further than the speaker ever could alone. Across borders. Across languages. Across time zones.

That discovery led to a body of work that grew beyond anything I had imagined. Music created from lived experience, purpose, and belief began circulating globally. Those tracks accumulated over 500 million streams across platforms. Albums reached number one positions on Amazon Music charts more than fourteen times. Invitations followed to speak, collaborate, and build projects around the world.

Yet the numbers were never the point.

The point was that ideas were moving.

When Words Wanted to Move

Speakers spend years refining their message. Authors labor over chapters that carry their life's work. Coaches repeat phrases that become mantras for their clients. Yet most of those words live briefly. They are spoken, heard, and then lost to memory.

Music does something different. It embeds language into the body. A chorus repeats until it becomes internal dialogue. A melody carries emotion long after the sound has stopped.

I began experimenting by placing spoken ideas into musical structure. Not as gimmick. As translation.

A speech has peaks and pauses. A story has tension and release. A belief has rhythm. When I aligned spoken wisdom with melody, something shifted. People remembered. They repeated. They shared.

What started as an experiment became a calling.

From Strategy to Sound

BrandStorming is not traditional branding. It does not begin with logos or taglines. It begins with identity.

Who are you becoming?
What do you stand for?
What do people feel when they encounter your message?

Music became the bridge between strategy and emotion. A brand could be explained, or it could be felt. When people feel something, they remember it. When they remember it, they act.

Masterminding sessions evolved into creative laboratories. A client would arrive with a book, a keynote, or a life's work. Through conversation, the essence would surface. Then it would be shaped into lyrics. Then into sound.

The result was not just content. It was a cultural asset. Something that could live on streaming platforms, at events, in campaigns, and inside communities.

The Global Echo

One of the quiet confirmations of discovering your gift is when the work no longer belongs to you alone.

Music created from these sessions began appearing in unexpected places. Played in offices. Used in training rooms. Shared at events. Listened to on long flights and early mornings.

Different accents. Different backgrounds. Same resonance.

That is when I understood that BrandStorming and music together were not a service. They were a system for unlocking expression.

People do not struggle because they lack knowledge. They struggle because they cannot translate what they know into something others can receive.

Sound solves that.

Elevating the Message

As invitations to speak increased, so did the responsibility to remain grounded in why the work mattered. Speaking on global stages is not about presence. It is about precision.

When you have minutes to reach people, clarity matters. Music trains you in that discipline. A song cannot ramble. It must land.

I began using music as a framing device for talks. Opening with sound. Closing with melody. Allowing audiences to leave with more than notes. They left with a feeling that stayed.

Clients noticed. Their own messages sharpened. Their delivery changed. Their confidence rose.

Not because they were louder. Because they were aligned.

What the Gift Requires

Every gift asks something of the person who carries it.

Mine requires listening more than speaking. It requires honoring other people's stories. It requires staying curious and unscripted.

BrandStorming cannot be automated. Masterminding cannot be rushed. Music cannot be forced.

The work demands presence. It demands trust. It demands the courage to let ideas evolve rather than control them.

That is why it continues to work across industries and cultures. It is human first.

Discover Your Gift

If there is one lesson this journey has taught me, it is this: your gift rarely arrives labelled.

It often hides inside the things you already do naturally. The conversations you enjoy. The patterns others come to you for help with. The moments when time disappears.

For me, it was seeing connections others missed. Hearing rhythm where others heard noise. Believing that ideas deserve more than one form.

By allowing BrandStorming, masterminding, and music to merge, I did not create something new. I uncovered what was already there.

Your gift may not look like mine. It does not need to.

But it will ask you the same question.

What happens when you stop separating your talents and allow them to speak to each other?

That is where discovery begins.

❋❋❋

Roy Smoothe

Good and Plenty

by Heidi Soos

My name is Heidi. This is my sweet soul's purpose story, and how the universe laid it out, again and again, until I truly took notice.

When I was a young child, Pop-pop time started at 5am, sitting on my grandfather's lap while he had his morning coffee. In my hands was a little black-and-white version of a book of dog breeds, already worn soft from use. I flipped the pages and gave commentary on my thoughts of them, often lingering on their faces. The ridiculous dog, the Brussels griffin. My favorites, the Labrador Retriever and the Golden Retriever. My grandfather watched me sometimes animated with laughter at the commentary, a knowing smile tugging at the corner of his mouth. He loved dogs, too. Always had.

In the breast pocket of his button-down shirt was an eyeglass case, and behind it, like a secret, was a small box of Good & Plenty or Good & Fruity candy. Every so often, he would reach in, pull one out, and place it in my palm. Not randomly. But intentionally. He was training me the way one trains a dog. Rewarding me, giving attention. I didn't know it then, but my nervous system was learning something ancient: trust, attunement, relationship understanding.

Both of my grandfathers loved animals, especially dogs. That love wrapped itself around me early, before I had language for it. It wasn't taught; it was transmitted. I felt it in my body in the way animals responded to me without effort. Dogs and horses, especially, seemed to recognize something familiar in me, as if we were speaking the same quiet dialect beneath words and complete vibes.

My passion for dogs was so obvious that, paradoxically, I denied it. I spent years searching for my life's work, my soul's purpose, convinced it had to be something more complex, impressive, more difficult to name. How does one make an honest living loving dogs? I couldn't comprehend how devotion translated into livelihood. Surely purpose had more definition and was more black-and-white.

I studied self-development, spirituality, healing, consciousness. I searched everywhere but the place that had been calling me since I was small enough to sit on my grandfather's lap. I was looking for revelation. What I didn't realize was that my soul had never stopped pointing in the same direction; I was just refusing to see it.

Years later, a friend of mine, Shajen, creator of *Discover the Gift*, introduced me to the Passion Test. The first time I took it, dogs appeared on the list, but I quietly dismissed it. The second time I took the test, I could not. There they were again, sitting with soft brown eyes, waiting for me to realize I could not live without them. When I finally allowed the truth to land, it felt less like discovering something new and more like remembering something generational.

Around that same time, I was attending shaman school, "Seeing with the Heart," immersed in years of journeying and soul work. During my rookie year, we journeyed to our soul's purpose. There was no metaphor, no symbol to decode. I was met with those soft brown eyes of a black dog. It was right there after calling in the four directions and grandmothers and grandfathers that a Powerful presence, guidance and my grandfather's true lineage.

After journeying to my soul's purpose, I wrote down all that I saw and stepped outside to integrate and contemplate, walking slowly into the natural world. As I stepped outside of the yurt and down the driveway, Raven and Shadow, my teacher Tracey's giant dogs, took their places, one under each of my hands. They walked beside me, steady and protective under each hand; they stayed as I floated. I felt Viking-strong, magnetized to the earth, rooted through my feet. I wept, not from sadness, but from recognition. I felt so tall, my chest swelling, and I floated down the driveway. Alpha pack leader embodied.

In that moment, I understood that dogs were not adjacent to my spiritual path. They were knit in my bones. They had always been my teachers in embodiment, presence, loyalty, and love. They had taught me leadership without force, intuition without fear, love without agenda.

Dogs brought me back into my body when spirituality tempted me to float away. They anchored me in responsibility, in stewardship, in care. They showed me that devotion is not abstract–it is daily, physical, and alive. It smells like fur and earth. It's soft and supple with a shot of oxytocin. It's those warm brown eyes.

What I once thought was "just a love of animals," revealed itself as a calling to work with life itself, to participate consciously in lineage, birth, presence, and relationship. To be in flow. To be alpha. To move energy. And watch a secret language.

I no longer question whether this is "worthy work" or a legitimate path. My soul answered that long ago, before I had words, before I had doubt. Purpose doesn't always arrive as lightning. Sometimes it sits patiently in your lap, offering you a book, a piece of candy, and a quiet knowing that you will one day remember who you are.

And when I did, everything finally made sense.

❋❋❋

Heidi Soos

Shamanic practitioner
Equilibrium midwife
Owner of Enlightened Labradors

soossmiles1111@gmail.com

Step Four: Infinite Feedback

Life Is Always Responding

> *"Life constantly provides feedback through experiences, relationships, and outcomes. When we reflect on these experiences with curiosity, the brain integrates emotional and cognitive information more effectively, allowing insight and learning to emerge. Feedback becomes a teacher when we listen."*

Nothing is wasted.

Every experience is feedback. What you call failure is often simply information. Research shows that reframing experience supports resilience and adaptive learning (Garland et al., 2017). When you stop judging outcomes and begin observing them, you gain access to insight. And insight creates growth.

Feedback is not punishment. It is guidance.

MEDITATION: LISTENING TO THE WISDOM OF YOUR LIFE

Take a slow breath in.
And gently let it go.

Life is always communicating with us.

Through joy.
Through challenge.
Through relationships.
Through endings and beginnings.
Through moments that stretch us and moments that bring us back home to ourselves again.

And yet many of us were never taught how to listen without judgment.

Instead, we resist.
We distract ourselves.
We numb.

We interpret experiences as punishment instead of information.

But what begins to happen when we slow down long enough to truly reflect is that life itself becomes a teacher.

Imagine yourself sitting beside still water.

As you gaze into it, reflections begin appearing across the surface. Conversations. Memories. Emotions. Patterns. Possibilities.

Not to shame you.
Not to criticize you.
But to invite awareness.

Infinite feedback reminds us that every experience carries information. Every moment offers us another opportunity to know ourselves more deeply.

And awareness itself changes the experience.

Sometimes healing begins simply by becoming honest with ourselves.

Ask yourself gently:

"What is life trying to show me right now?"

And then listen.

Not critically.
Not defensively.
But openly.

Research in emotional intelligence and mindfulness consistently shows that self-awareness is foundational to growth, resilience, emotional regulation, and healthy relationships.

The more aware we become, the more consciously we begin living.

Quietly repeat:

"I am willing to listen."
"Every experience carries wisdom."
"I grow through awareness."
"I trust the unfolding of my life."

Take another breath.

And remember that life is not happening against you.

In many ways, it is continually inviting you into deeper awareness, deeper compassion, and deeper understanding of yourself and others.

"To me, the ultimate Gift that one person can give to another is inspiration. Inspiration is an energy, a wave form. When we're in that perfect frequency of what we're supposed to be doing, we can get into a state of perpetual chills going up and down our back. A perpetual state of inspiration."

DAVID "AVOCADO" WOLFE

The Gift of Pain to Discover Joy

by Melissa Tori

What did you want to be when you grew up? Imagine the one thing you wanted most in life, and the universe tells you, "No."

Hi, I'm Melissa Tori, inspirational speaker, truth guide, international best-selling author...a person with gifts who took the better part of her life finding. But before any of that, I was a woman who believed one dream would save her.

A quick look back reveals understanding that joy isn't something you earn, but something you allow; it is a life shift that is only discovered through time, pain, self-love, healing and growth. I thought joy arrived once life finally looked the way it was supposed to, the way society says it should look: husband, wife and children - a family unit.

All my life, all I ever wanted to be was a wife and mother. I wrapped my worth and value into being a mom, believing that was the way to be chosen, valued, and seen.

When that life didn't happen, it was more than a loss - it was a complete identity collapse.

Divorced at 32 with no children, it seemed my dreams would not be realized. I honestly believed that some people were put on this earth to suffer, so others won't have to, and I truly believed I was one of those people.

It wasn't just the loss of my marriage; it was the loss of the life I believed would make me whole. This dream wasn't simply desire. It was a promise I made to myself, that if I did life correctly, the pain and turmoil of a chaotic childhood would stop. That story told me who I was allowed to be, what made me valuable, and how joy would eventually arrive.

Accepting a plan for my life I didn't want or desire left me empty, hopeless, less than. There is a particular kind of pain that comes from not having a child. It does not go away. There is always an ache. A quiet, persistent, "Why not me?" It bled into all aspects of my life, professionally, personally, and deeply emotionally. I didn't know who I was.

One of the hardest parts is that the world keeps going as your life takes an unconventional turn. There is little sympathy from those who cannot understand your invisible grief.

I became very good at pretending I was fine out of fear of scaring people off. Carrying pain alone and in silence, I learned how to smile through conversations about children.

I began believing that joy belonged to everyone else. That belief kept me stuck. I believed that I was meant to endure life, not enjoy it. I remained in toxic situations, feared leaving jobs after being mistreated, overcompensated in personal relationships to earn love and belonging.

My coping mechanism? Food, which turned into a full-on addiction. Food didn't yell or judge or leave. It didn't reject me. It was safe and predictable. It was my only friend.

Approaching 40, I'd settled into life as a single woman. I'd made a few friends, distracted myself with work, but slowly realized that I wasn't living: I was surviving. I quietly hoped no one would see how small and empty my life had become.

At 44 years old and 320+ pounds, I hated everything about myself and my life.

Everything changed the day after Christmas 2014. I was sitting alone on the couch at 10:30 in the morning with a half-gallon of ice cream in my lap, eating it straight from the container. I stopped and said, "What are you doing? Seriously, what are you doing? If you don't change something, you're going to be dead before you're 50."

In that moment, I made a decision…to take back my life!

I knew I couldn't go back and repair the past, but I was learning I could heal from it. I could grow past it. And in that growth, I became open to new dreams and new possibilities. I learned to love and accept myself for who I was.

What if the thing you've been waiting for is actually waiting for you?

Choosing myself was a slow burn at first. It didn't feel empowering; in fact, it felt almost unbearable. How does a person take a lifetime of putting themself last to then putting themself first? How does one begin to take the excuses they accepted, and shift them into the reasons they can no longer be who they used to be?

One small decision at a time. And each time we choose ourselves, we are choosing joy, whether we realize it or not. These choices do not erase the grief, remove the ache of childlessness, or make life suddenly fair. What they do is open a door.

Fast forward to 55 years old, after losing 195 pounds naturally, I learned how to love every version of myself by showing up every day.

My goal is not to highlight my weight loss; rather, my intention is to model that real transformation is possible when we show up for ourselves. It's not about what we achieve; it's about who we become.

I stopped believing that happiness was something earned after an appropriate amount of suffering and started believing that joy was available if I allowed it. The thing about joy is this: it's only elusive if you push it away.

Joy comes in many forms, and most don't announce themselves. For me, joy looks like movement that honors my body and my journey, quiet mornings where I keep promises to myself, and celebrating the small wins I used to dismiss without thought. It's smiling at someone, knowing you might be the only kindness they see that day.

Joy means different things to different people, and that truth reshaped my understanding of it.

What does joy look like for you in your life right now?

Let's be honest … my dream didn't come true. But I found a way to live a dream life anyway. And that distinction matters.

If you are grieving a life that never showed up for you, I would like you know:

- The pain may never fully go away

- The ache will still visit from time to time
- There will be questions that remain unanswered

But you are still allowed to:

- Choose yourself first
- Build a life with meaning
- Experience joy

And not later or once your healing is complete, but right now, with the life you are living today.

Loving myself enough to choose me, whatever that looked like in each season, became the key that unlocked my happiness, contentment, peace, and a life that felt worthy.

We are all one decision away from a completely different circumstance. We get to control our destiny. These choices, made quietly, over and over, are exactly how joy becomes possible. And it is possible for you.

This story is a small piece of my bigger journey. I share more, along with backstory and truths I've learned along the way, in my upcoming book, *Allowed to Choose.* This is for anyone wanting to continue the exploration of what's possible when you choose to show up for yourself.

MELISSA TORI

You can find me online at **www.melissatori.com** and **@melissatori** on most socials. If you're navigating your own journey of self-discovery, and you're ready for support around it, this is what I do. Let's connect.

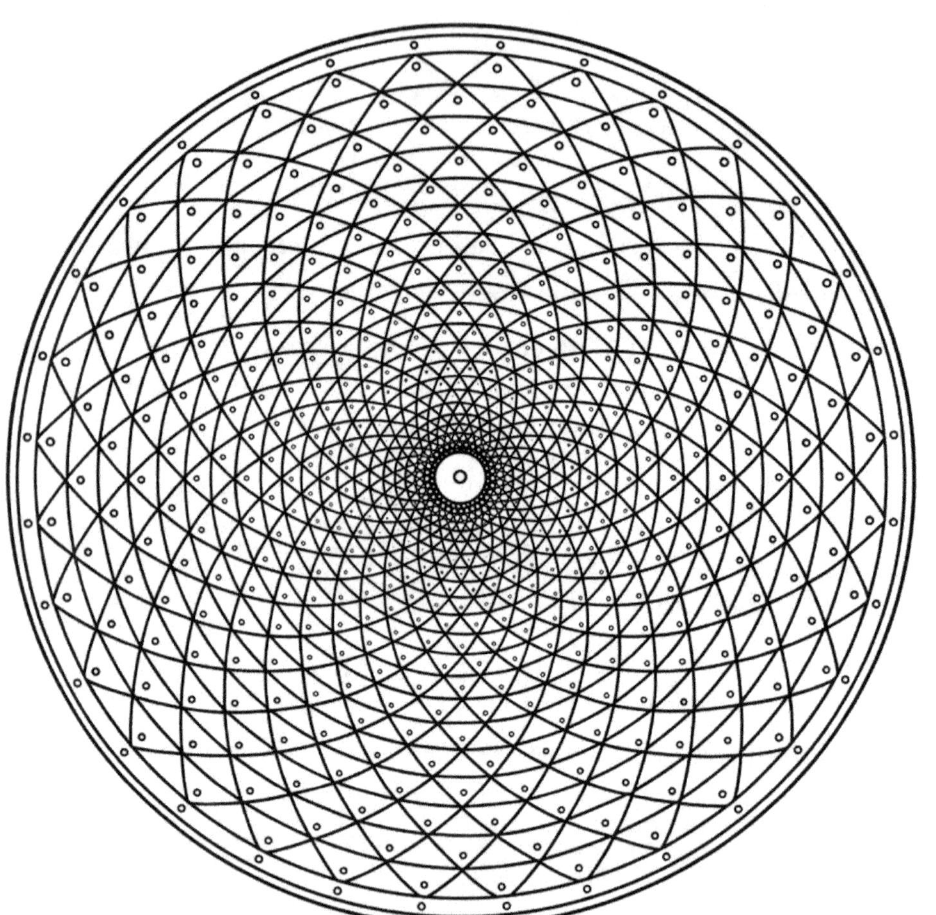

THE JOURNEY STARTS WITH YOU

BY DR. RANDY SCHAETZKE, D.C., D.I.B.A.K.

Being a Doctor of Chiropractic Medicine and a Professional Applied Kinesiology, I have experienced people from all walks of life and in all states of pain and functionality.

I have always said that discovering your gift is one of the most important journeys you will ever take. And the funny thing is, most people think their gift is something "out there," something they have to chase down, earn, or stumble into. But in reality, your gift is usually something simple, something already woven into who you are. The challenge is clearing away enough of the noise to actually see it.

Life has a way of getting complicated. The more you learn, the more you think, the more you try to manage, the more tangled things can become. You set a direction, you think the road is paved and straight, and then suddenly you are on a Class 4 road, wondering how you got there. I have been on plenty of those roads, literally and figuratively. They are bumpy, unpredictable, sometimes frustrating, but they are also where the real adventure happens.

And here is the thing: we often create our own obstacles. Not because we are trying to sabotage ourselves, but because human beings crave sensation. We crave challenge. We crave drama. Drama makes us feel alive, even the negative kind. It is like a biochemical jolt. Stress hormones fire, the nervous system lights up, and suddenly we are "in it." It is not always healthy, but it is familiar. News programs and many movies play on this need for drama; they know it and sell it to us, and we buy it, again and again.

But is that the best way to feel alive? Of course not. It is just the most common way.

When life gets complicated, the smartest thing you can do is look for simplicity underneath it. Every complex system, whether it is anatomy, physiology, nutrition, or chemistry, has a simple foundation. Once you understand that foundation, the complexity stops being overwhelming. It becomes manageable. It becomes clear, so keep it simple. You know the old adage, "less is more?" The same is true for your life.

When you reconnect with the simplicity of who you are, your whole physiology shifts. Your vibration changes, and yes, I use that word intentionally. Thoughts create measurable physiological changes. Think about something stressful, and your body responds instantly. Think about something uplifting, and your chemistry shifts just as fast. That is not magic. That is neurology, hormones, and the innate intelligence of your body doing what it is designed to do.

One of the tricks I use myself is going back to a time when

everything felt aligned, when life was flowing, when I felt strong, capable, energized. I revisit that feeling, that vibration, and I ask myself:

What was I doing then that I am not doing now? Because if it worked once, it could work again. We forget. We drift. Sometimes we need to remind ourselves who we were before the noise crept in.

Another practice I use, and I will admit, it is not easy, is trying to stop thinking inward. Do not stop thinking entirely but stop narrating. Stop labeling. Stop talking to yourself in your head. When you were an infant, you had feelings without language. You experienced the world directly. There is purity in that, a clarity. When I can get even 20 seconds of that quiet, it resets me. It is like hitting the reboot button on the nervous system.

And then there is the beach ball analogy. You are in a pool, chasing a beach ball, splashing, and kicking, trying to grab it, and all you are doing is pushing it farther away. But the moment you stop struggling, the moment you relax, the waves settle, and the beach ball drifts right back to you. Sometimes the fastest way forward is to stop forcing things.

Discovering your gift matters, and it is not about adding more. It is about peeling away the layers that are not you. It is about quieting the noise long enough to hear your own inner intelligence. It is about remembering that you do not have to struggle to be yourself.

When you reconnect with that authenticity, with your honest nature, you feel it immediately. You smile for no reason. You breathe easier. You feel aligned. And that is when you know you are doing something right.

That is when you know you are being *you*, and if I learned anything in my time on this earth, being a healer and doing the work of Discover the Gift, it is, stated, you *are* the gift. So, take care of yourself in the best ways you know how. You are the only you on this planet.

When your body is trying to tell you something, even if it seems like it is betraying you, STOP and listen, breath like a baby, let your shoulders drop, let your stomach relax and expand with your breath. This changes your physical stress on your body, and it changes your pH and chemistry of your body in a minute. Take the time to relax and breathe.

While you are at that, think, "What else could I do for myself in a positive way?" One option would be to nourish yourself in a way that makes you smile. I'm not just talking about eating some chocolate cake that makes you happy (that's OK!) but the point here is to do something that nourishes yourself and you know it supports your well-being, yet at the same time, makes you smile.

Doesn't it just irk you sometimes about people who love to exercise? I don't love exercising. I do it, but I don't love it, but I love how it makes me feel, so I do it. I don't always do any extensive exercise. Sometimes I'll make a deal with myself: *I'll watch this television program, and during the commercial I'm going to do some push-ups or I'll do some planks or both; you know, it's only a couple of minutes long and then you're done.*

Accomplishment feels good, to do something that you can accomplish in a short time that's positive for you and wasn't a burden, and then you can look back and say, "I did it! Good for me!" And 30 minutes later, you can do it again. If I'm really tired and I know I should do something physical, I will just do some simple stretches on the floor in the living room; simple yoga stretches work fine for me. What works for you, just do it.

The Journey Starts with You. Stay active; your body will thank you.

❋❋❋

Dr. Randy Schaetzke, D.C., D.I.B.A.K.

Don't hesitate to contact me at
(802) 296-6030
www.doctorrandy.com

The Frequency of Joy

by Dianne Callahan

I'm Dianne. I'm a best-selling author, keynote speaker, radio show host, mastermind leader, and philanthropist. I'm also a tough warrior and 4-time cancer survivor. My passion is helping women break free of imposter syndrome by reclaiming their inner 6-year-old in a Wonder Woman cape and showing up with unshakeable self-confidence.

Before you read another word, I want you to take a moment to imagine. Close your eyes and think back to old episodes of The Waltons, or maybe old movies set in the first half of the last century. What's one thing you can see sitting proudly in the living room? It's an old-timey radio.

Curved at the top, fancy or plain. It's not small; it's more like a piece of furniture. The cabinet is crafted from burnished wood that has softened a bit with age. If you run your hand along its surface, you can feel the smoothness worn in by decades of fingertips turning knobs, resting palms, quiet evenings gathered round. It has a gentle warmth, and you know it remembers every story it has ever told.

At the center is the dial.

A round glass window, slightly fogged at the edges. Its amber light glows from within, illuminating numbers like a promise of wonderful things waiting to be found. The light seems to hum faintly, alive. Persistent. Present for you.

You reach for the knob. It resists just a little; metal cool beneath your fingers, ridged for grip, reassuringly real. When you turn it, the room fills with the sound of static. This is the in-between, the moment before clarity. The reminder that something is there, even if you can't quite hear it yet.

And then, a click.
A subtle shift.

Music drifts through the speaker's cloth, rich and rounded, as if it has traveled a long way to reach you. A swing band brings lighthearted energy to the room with brass and rhythm, trumpets lifting the air, a stand-up bass walking steadily beneath it all. The sound isn't sharp or perfect; it's textured, slightly fuzzy at the edges, like velvet rubbed the wrong way. It wraps around you instead of striking you. It feels *felt*, not just heard.

As you listen, you notice something else.

The radio never strains.
It never searches frantically.
It simply receives and shares.

The music was always there.
The signal never left.

All that changed was the tuning.

Joy, you realize, is like this.

Not something to chase.
Not something to manufacture.
Not something reserved for special moments or lucky people.

Joy is a frequency: steady, constant, quietly broadcasting, ready for you to tune in, anytime, anyplace.

When I imagine that radio, I can "see" the musical notes set free from the wooden shell. I see them floating up, up, up into the air, light as a feather, or a balloon. Or bubbles. Yes, bubbles of joy!

In her 2019 book, "Joyful: The Surprising Power of Ordinary Things to Create Extraordinary Happiness," author Ingrid Fetell Lee set out to understand how the physical world influences our emotions and why certain things spark joy. Through hundreds of conversations, she noticed repeatedly that some tangible things were universally joyful.

Things like bubbles.
Rainbows.
Beach balls.
Swimming pools and treehouses and fireworks.
Hot air balloons and ice cream sundaes with colorful sprinkles.

"Joy isn't hard to find," she wrote, "In fact, it's all around us."

I agree. But sometimes, the beautiful notes of joy are muffled, the colors muted. The sound turns to static, and the colors melt together into a dull grey blob. When life feels heavy or silent, it is not because joy has disappeared. It is because the dial has been nudged. Because static has crept in.

I help women tune into their joy by turning down the static and returning to their "factory settings" of self-confidence and self-esteem. What I have seen in their lives and in my own is that human self-confidence is much like the banks of a swiftly flowing river, easily eroded by its surroundings.

Social media. Societal norms of beauty. Family expectations. The environment we grow up in. Comparison. Competition. The ugly and mean words of others, especially those who are supposed to love us. How do we hope to remain the self-loving, brave, and joyful person we were born to be?

According to research by A Mighty Girl, between the ages of 8 and 14, girls' confidence levels nosedive by 30%. And it gets worse as we get older. In a recent study by Gitnux, 85% of people worldwide suffer from low self-esteem, affecting their work and life potential.

I don't just report those statistics, I've lived them. I've always been the heavyset girl, and let me tell you, the bullying, excluding, and name-calling started early. Year by year, it wore away at my natural confidence and exuberance. When I was 17, I dared to think the cute guy from school who came into my place of work and wanted to "hang out" after my shift was actually interested in me. Turns out, what he was interested in was parking in a dark field and forcing me to have sex with him while he yelled at me to stop crying.

That date rape led to me marrying someone with an anger issue who demanded that I lose weight and said cruel things to me while swearing he loved me, which led to me standing in my en suite bathroom holding a gun to my head on a sunny Sunday morning. Broken? Self-loathing? Worthless? Never good enough? I've lived all those secret feelings, even while I was succeeding in my career and keeping my family in the dark about what was really going on.

When we don't feel worthy, when we cannot see our own value as a human being, joy seems very far away. But I promise you, no matter how you feel today, you are worthy. You are strong and beautiful, wise and brave. You've overcome things that most people can't even imagine.

Here's what I know: if I can rebuild my confidence and self-worth, you can too. Below are three practices that have helped me reclaim my inner 6-year-old in a Wonder Woman cape and return to the joyful, confident human I was born to be. (Warning: it doesn't happen overnight - it's a lifelong operation.)

1. Practice replacing negative thoughts with kinder words. Ask, "Is this even true? Says who?"

2. Stop outsourcing your worth. Look for things you love about yourself; don't rely on other people's comments or opinions to fuel your self-value.

3. Engineer micro wins and celebrate yourself. Your brain believes who you repeatedly tell it you are. That's neuroscience.

But remember, joy isn't a reward for doing the work. It's yours, right this minute. The frequency of joy is always there, ready to fill our hearts, bless our lives, and turn our eyes skyward. The signal is still playing. The music has not stopped. The bubbles are just waiting for us to look up and notice them.

And you, right now, are learning how to tune back in.

❋❋❋

DIANNE CALLAHAN is an international best-selling author; her books "Journey Through Illness: The Ultimate Guidebook for a Trip You Never Thought You'd Take" and "Lighthearted Life: Simple Strategies to Live a Joy-filled Life Even in the Stormiest

Times" are available on Amazon and at DianneMCallahan.com. Visit her website for speaking and partnership inquiries. Dianne's passion is encouraging people to Live Urgently every day. For joyful inspiration, join Dianne's Facebook group Lighthearted Life Community.

> Dianne Callahan can be found at **www.diannemcallahan.com** for speaking inquiries and book sales.
>
> For joyful inspiration and connection, join Dianne's **Lighthearted Life Community** on Facebook.

Step Five: Vibration

Your Internal State Shapes Your Experience

> *"Our emotional states influence how we experience the world. Practices such as gratitude, compassion, and mindful awareness activate neural circuits associated with positive emotional regulation. These emotional states support resilience and well-being."*

Your internal state is not separate from your external life. It shapes it. Emotional and physiological systems influence perception and behavior (Kok et al., 2017). When you shift internally... your experience shifts.

Alignment creates coherence. And coherence creates clarity.

Meditation: Becoming Conscious of the Energy You Carry

Close your eyes.
Take a slow breath in.
And gently exhale.

Everything is energy.

Your thoughts.
Your words.
Your attention.
Your emotional state.
Your presence.

And whether we realize it or not, we are constantly affecting the emotional environments around us.

Bring your awareness now to your heart center.

Imagine a warm field of light surrounding you, expanding softly with every breath.

Notice what happens when you slow down.
Notice what happens when you choose gratitude.
Notice how compassion changes the way your body feels.

The nervous system responds to repeated emotional states. What we practice consistently becomes more familiar neurologically, emotionally, and behaviorally.

And this matters deeply.

Not because we should force positivity or pretend to feel joyful all the time.

But because awareness gives us choice.

You see, joy is rarely something we force ourselves into. More often, joy begins emerging naturally when we create internal conditions of presence, safety, connection, meaning, and alignment.

Sometimes joy arrives quietly.

In a breath.
In laughter.
In feeling understood.
In the sunlight moving across a room.
In the realization that despite everything, your heart is still capable of opening.

Take another breath.

And ask yourself softly:

"What energy do I want to contribute to my life and to the lives of those around me today?"

Quietly repeat:

"I cultivate peace within myself."
"My energy matters."
"I choose awareness and compassion."
"I create space for joy to emerge naturally."

And perhaps vibration is not about perfection at all.

Perhaps it is simply about becoming conscious enough to notice what we are cultivating within ourselves and within the world around us.

"There's an awakening that's happening; there's a quickening that is happening right now. This is the most exciting time. It is such an exciting time because we each have the ability to bring out, ALLOW, and be receptive to that which is your very life. To flow and in that space, to shine."

NIURKA

MASTER TRAINER OF NEUROLINGUISTIC PROGRAMMING MEMBER, AMERICAN BOARD OF NLP & HYPNOTHERAPY, AUTHOR

The Joy and Freedom in Authenticity

by Kim Somers Egelsee

I'm Kim Somers Egelsee, a wife, a mom of two daughters, co-founder of Publishing Joy, bestselling author, TEDx speaker, intuitive and coach. I love to help women tune into their true authentic selves, love themselves completely, and let out their unique gifts to the world.

The real power lies in letting our truth, our raw authentic self out to the world. This is freedom.

It took me a long time to shed my ego and step into the most authentic version of myself. Starting at a young age, after being bullied by the neighborhood kids at age 9 and being declared one of the ugliest girls in the class by the boys in 6th grade, my confidence had taken a plunge. This resulted in large efforts to wear more make up, dress more impressively, and try harder to get friends to like and accept me, all the while not feeling secure or complete.

I spent high school feeling confident and authentic, but still trying hard to be liked or popular, and never feeling quite like I measured up. I always just felt mediocre. As I got older, I actually believed that I was one of those people who was just average at everything. I had never won awards, never received accolades or recognition, and always got small parts in the shows. I continued on my life path to pursue acting, going into auditions trying to mold into what they wanted or thought I should be. I did some acting, modeling, and ended up leaving a very toxic love relationship.

Afterward, I met the love of my life, and at that young age of 22, began deeper work on myself. It was a very long process, with many rollercoaster bumps, shake ups and upsets. I got caught up in image, appearance and the world of entertainment in my late twenties, and realized I was feeling off, unfulfilled and not true to myself. I also had just lost my grandma, who was a second mom to me, and I didn't handle that well.

I realized that I was losing myself. Did I really know myself deeply? Was I living a life true to who I wanted to be and become? How did I get here? I made the decision to talk to a therapist, and to research, study and immerse myself in reading about spirituality, consciousness, confidence, and leadership. I started seeing a holistic doctor and shaman who became my mentor. Soon, I realized that I could use my intuitive gifts (and my college degree) to do readings and life coaching for people. The journey continued, and as I learned how to shed my ego, I stepped more and more into the freedom of being my authentic self, while simultaneously learning how to do so. I got more certifications and credentials in Educational Psychology and decided to make it my career. It was my purpose; helping others feel this way and experience life so magically too.

I studied why we as humans don't just automatically live authentically, real, raw and vulnerable. I found that many times, we don't even realize we aren't our true selves, until we are unhappy, moody or unfulfilled. We often don't feel safe to be ourselves, for fear of being judged, ridiculed or even potentially losing chances at something. We try to fit the mold of a perfect, ideal person due to expectations from loved ones or what we think that society wants from us. We also aren't sure how to change. Some of us have gotten so good at being fake, that we don't even know ourselves on a deeper level.

I also discovered ways that we can evolve into the best, real versions of self. I applied all of these, and it got me to a place of peace, authenticity, vulnerability, and truth. We need to do the deep, healing work. This can consist of inner child healing, somatic, trauma healing, therapy, work on limiting beliefs, and more. The practice of telling your truth, setting strong boundaries, and eliminating any people pleasing. It even involves wearing things that make you feel you, alive, and amazing. It is important to realize that you are safe, there are people who love you for you, you have a home, gifts, abilities, unique qualities, and it's okay if some people don't resonate with you. We don't have space and energy for everyone.

> *"This above all: to thine own self be true, and it must follow, as the night the day Thou canst not then be false to any man."*
> – William Shakespeare

Finally, I live and experience the results of this work on my consciousness, confidence, ego death, and stepping into my joy and freedom as my genuine bona fide "me." These are the results and why it's so worth the work. I started naturally to stand out from the crowd. There aren't many people living totally honestly, so I stand out. I feel this indescribable sense of freedom. I love myself more because I'm no longer betraying my inner child or true self, therefore I feel more joyful. I attract other genuine people to me. I make clearer decisions. I feel so divinely connected and guided and get to be 100% me.

You can do this, too! Practice having the courage to be vulnerable and in your truth. Decide that this year, you will let go of anything that doesn't feel 100% aligned with your heart and soul, which makes space for greatness. Ask yourself: if the person you have the potential to become met who you are now, what would they tell you to do? You only live once, and you owe it to yourself to be authentic, free, and filled with joy.

Snails, turtles and clams have shells, not humans. Take yours off and have the nerve to be yourself.

❋❋❋

KIM SOMERS EGELSEE

Manifesting the Dream

by Larissa Michelle Pollica

Namaste. My name is Larissa; most people call me Lara, and I am a healer. Being a healer does not mean you are fully healed; very few people in human history have reached a state of complete self-actualization. To be a healer is to be conscious of your own healing journey and to be moved to assist actualization, assisting others on theirs. We are all wonderful yet imperfect works in progress, continually learning how to return to wholeness. My life's course has been braided from caregiving, grief, discovery, and ultimately, the reclamation of joy.

For most of my life, I have been employed as a critical care nurse, devoted to my patients within the concrete walls of corporate medicine. Those years taught me discipline, clinical judgment, and the quiet art of presence. They also taught me how systems can erode the human spirit when profit and efficiency eclipse compassion. Lately, with great enthusiasm, my career path has been evolving. The candle of my passion has been lit and now burns with a steady, warm glow.

So many people work and live lives they do not enjoy. I know because I was one of them. Nurses, and this applies to many in a caregiving service (medical providers, first responders, teachers, and mothers), are often unappreciated, underpaid, and overworked. Our society would collapse without nurturers and caregivers, yet our crucial role is undervalued. Nursing is inseparable from empathy, love, and self-sacrifice, but the prevailing stereotype of the ideal nurse and the enduring myth of self-sacrifice have driven many of us to utter exhaustion.

Ironically, nurses are expected to advocate health, promoting behaviors for patients while simultaneously being expected to sacrifice our own basic needs. Harsh working conditions, increasingly complex patient care requirements, chronic staff shortages, physical job demands, being pushed beyond reasonable limits, fatigue, workplace violence, feelings of helplessness, horizontal hostility among disempowered colleagues, toxic work environments, insufficient support from management and administration, and pay not commensurate with our valuable contribution, all lead to depersonalization and burnout. And yet nurses keep showing up, all night, on weekends, holidays, through snowstorms, because caring is not just what we do; it is who we are. Meanwhile, the healthcare industry capitalizes on our goodness.

Despite these systemic challenges, nursing has gifted me with a deep, embodied knowing. I cherish the talented nurses and compassionate doctors who taught me how to assess, how to listen, and how to hold presence in moments that matter. Over the years, I have had the honor of helping bring babies into the world, as well as facilitating dying, the transition out of this plane of existence in dignity and comfort. Those intimate moments taught me more about the human spirit than any textbook ever could. They also revealed the limits of a system that treats people as a diagnosis and problems to be fixed rather than whole beings to be held.

What I learned is that modern medicine's pendulum has swung too far toward technology, pharmaceuticals, and a focus on disease rather than the whole person. The Western medical model treats the physical body with pills and procedures, quick fixes that often ignore the deeper cause of illness. This high-tech, low-touch standard has overshadowed essential elements of human care and simple common sense. Prevention, clean eating and adequate hydration, movement, stress reduction, lifestyle, mental health, positive social interaction, spirituality, natural alternatives, the mindbody connection, and getting to the root of wellness for long-term health are too often glossed over in clinical encounters. There certainly is a time and place for science and technology; yet we are integrated beings, and you cannot separate the physical body from mind and spirit.

By late 2021, I had reached a debilitating state of depletion. The death of both of my parents, followed by the intensity of nursing in the COVID-19 pandemic's epicenter, had taken a heavy toll. My body was breaking down, my nervous system was dysregulated, and grief overwhelmed me. I felt like I was drowning. It was in that darkness, paradoxically, that I discovered a beacon of hope and existential growth.

Seeking the soothing sun and ocean, I eloped to the remote island of Vieques, Puerto Rico, where the nirvana of the Caribbean Sea received me. As the saying goes, "There ain't nothing salt water can't cure: sweat, tears, and the ocean." With the help of Paso Fino horses, riding in the serene waves on the most spectacular beaches in the world, I let go of remorse for all the mistakes I have made. Paddleboarding my way around the island with my little stray surfer dog, Zorro, we floated on the translucent sapphire- and aquamarine-colored ocean's surface, which shimmered in the sunlight like a million little diamonds. Then I would swim off the board with my snorkel beneath the sun's dappled surface into a warm, breathtaking alternate universe in the living tapestry of coral reef, where turtles, starfish, and stingrays thrived in the vibrant swaying ecosystem. Plucking ripe, juicy, delicious papaya and mango off the trees, we wandered the salty beaches and collected hundreds of shells which I converted into mosaic art. Gradually, my nervous system rebooted, and layers of grief and stress were washed away. With the power of the tide, energy moving as water through my body, I acquiesced to the flood of tears which cleansed me. Letting go of what no longer served me allowed a whole new wave of bliss to flow in.

There was a paradigm shift. I had an epiphany: we must replace the culture of self-sacrifice with a culture of self-care. It seems obvious, but I had to physically remove myself from my former environment and fully embrace island time to see it. The key to unlocking an authentic life is a simple concept that so many of us stray from, due to the demands of modern society and the disconnect it brings. To live in alignment with the essence of who you are, an instrumental method can be adopted to give energy to the things you love and minimize devoting time to the things that don't resonate with your soul's purpose. I didn't want to leave Vieques–the mermaid lifestyle immersed in nature, art, sunset beach yoga, music, horses, and freedom gave me an at-oneness I was not willing to depart from. The experience was so profound that I wanted to share it and lead others to the sacrosanct healing the island provides.

Buoyed by a clear vision, I was motivated to develop a curated reproduction of my metamorphosis to share through transformative retreat experiences. I realized it might be possible to earn a living doing what I loved, combining clinical insight with holistic practices and a wide variety of paradise inspired methods, to help seekers reclaim balance and health. A series of events then unfolded which felt like divine intervention, synchronicity, and a little good luck sprinkled in. A family moving to St. Croix offered to sell me a property in the blessed barrio of Santa Maria and endorsed my vision. A philanthropist on the island believed in the visionary concept and offered financial support. Thus, Passionflower Transformative Wellness Healing Arts Center (Passionflower) was born.

With reverence for the land and deep respect for its people, I set out to bring my vision to life. I am driven to offer an alternative path that emphasizes natural wellness, selfcare, and peace. There is still much work to be done, but I am in a productive flow state because I reclaimed my power. I am not having an anxiety attack in the hospital parking lot before my dreaded shift. I wake up with purpose at Passionflower, my spirit energized and ready for the day's adventure.

We have planted hundreds of tropical trees, plants, and herbs: a lush, edible landscape providing a fragrant pause that connects the soul to the earth. How good it feels to have my hands in the clay, growing flowers and fruit to nourish future retreat guests! At night, within Passionflower's humble wood walls, surrounded by medicinal plants and lulled by chirps of coquí frogs and the nearby ocean's soothing roar, I fall asleep filled with bliss.

Following your passion is not always a piece of cake. It is terrifying to leave behind a stable job you have been conditioned to accept as what you are supposed to do. To take a leap of faith, you have to jump. Passionflower has given me the opportunity to put all of my gifts into practice and to build a network of like-minded people who have already changed lives. When one person engages in self-awareness and conscious evolution, the ripple effect lifts entire families and communities. I dream that my true love will partner with me on this mission, magnify the progress, and prove that "happily ever after" is not simply a fairy tale. Passionflower is the culmination of my life's work, my truth, my intangible impact, and the Eden I will leave for my beloved daughters.

❋❋❋

Larissa Michelle Pollica, BSN, RN, CEN

Passionflowerwellness.com

Step Six: Adversity and Transformation

The Gift Within the Challenge

> *"Challenges often stimulate growth. Research on resilience and post-traumatic growth shows that individuals can develop greater strength, empathy, and purpose through adversity. When we reflect on difficult experiences with openness, the brain begins to integrate those experiences into a broader sense of meaning."*

Adversity is not the end of the path. It is part of it.

Growth emerges through meaning-making (Wu et al., 2019). Not avoidance. Transformation happens when experience becomes integrated.

Meditation: Honoring the Wisdom Within Your Journey

Take a slow breath in.
And gently let it go.

You have lived through moments that changed you.

Moments that stretched you.
Moments that hurt deeply.
Moments that challenged your understanding of yourself, of others, and of life itself.

And yet here you are.

Still breathing.
Still learning.
Still becoming.

Sometimes adversity dismantles the versions of ourselves built entirely around survival. And while painful, what emerges afterward can hold extraordinary depth, compassion, resilience, wisdom, and humanity.

Transformation rarely happens all at once.

More often, it unfolds quietly.

Moment by moment.
Choice by choice.
Breath by breath.

Imagine yourself standing after a storm has passed. The air feels clearer now. The ground renewed. Something within you wiser and more grounded than before.

Not because suffering is required for growth.

But because human beings possess an extraordinary capacity to heal, adapt, and evolve.

Research in resilience and post-traumatic growth continues to affirm that adversity, when met with support, reflection, connection, and meaning-making, can deepen empathy and increase our capacity for awareness and compassion.

The nervous system remembers pain.
But it also remembers safety.
It remembers kindness.
It remembers healing.
It remembers love.

Take another breath.

And honor yourself.

Not only for your successes.
But for your willingness to continue despite everything you

have lived through.

Quietly repeat:

"I honor my strength."
"I trust my ability to heal and grow."
"My pain is not the end of my story."
"I allow transformation to unfold naturally."

And perhaps for just this moment, allow yourself to acknowledge how far you have already come.

> *"Adversity is the diamond dust Heaven polishes its jewels with."*

THOMAS CARLYLE

MIRACLES IN ACTION

BY ANGELA ALEXANDER

My name is Angela Alexander. I'm an author, inspirational speaker, and a co-producer of my documentary film "*Miracles in Action*." God transitioned me from military to ministry so I could retire from the Air Force and share this incredible testimony.

During the second year of my marriage, I clearly remember Doctor Klara saying, "You'll probably be a widow by Christmas." It was only December 3rd.

The day before, my husband, Surie, had an excruciating headache. He couldn't speak, read, or write. Surie had suffered a severe brain aneurysm at age 24 while he was in the Army. We were evacuated from Germany to Walter Reed Hospital in Washington D.C., where he underwent an 18-hour brain surgery. When he awakened, the only phrases he would say were, "*I love you,*" "*You're beautiful,*" and "*Give me kisses.*" He stayed in the hospital for eight months. Despite his daily therapy sessions, he still Introduced me as his husband, Angela. Due to his medical condition, Surie was honorably and medically retired.

Eventually, we had two children named Angela and Murice. We were so grateful that Surie not only survived that brain aneurysm but also had his quality of life. We were thankful that Surie had regained his independence. In the spirit of giving back, we decided to become a Foster Care family. Within a few months, our family grew from two children to four, with the addition of Angelina and Reggie.

While I was in Japan on military duty, my husband and our four children were in a fatal car crash. Our car fell 25 feet off a highway and landed upside down on top of two parked cars, which had people inside. Praise God, our car fell on their engines and not their roofs. The people in the vehicles were extremely shaken up, but they were alright.

The police, firefighters, and paramedics arrived. An officer asked my 11-year-old daughter Angela, who was in and out of consciousness, "Where's your mother?" She said, "My mother is in Japan." The officer assumed she had hit her head too hard and was confused.

Surie sustained a concussion. An officer heard his voice, which was instantly slurred again, and assumed he was under the influence of drugs. They were prepared to take him straight to jail. Angela said, "No, stop right there! My father had a brain aneurysm!" However, she lost credibility when she said I was in Japan, leading them to doubt her statements entirely. The officers retrieved our address from Surie's driver's license and came to our home. No one answered. A neighbor informed the officer that I was in Japan.

It was the weekend of April Fool's Day. Lieutenant Mivehchi approached and summoned me from the group. We entered a small office; inside was a man who was introduced as a priest, and a female from our unit. The priest began nervously reading paperwork from the Red Cross. He said, "Angela, your family has been in a car accident." From the looks on their faces, I knew this was no April Fool's joke.

The Priest said, "Your husband, Surie, he's in the hospital, but he's okay."

"Your daughter, Angela, she's in the hospital, but she's okay."

"Your daughter, Angelina, she's in the hospital, but she's okay."

"Your two eight-year-old sons, Murice and Reggie, they didn't make it."

Instantly, I recalled a prayer my children said before going to bed.

Now I lay me down to sleep,

I pray the Lord my soul to keep.

If I should die before I wake,

I pray the Lord my soul to take.

I felt in my heart as if I heard them say, "No, Mommy, that priest is wrong! We prayed the Lord our souls to take. We did make it; we're here with J-e-s-u-s!"

God was sending me so much love and so much peace. The people in the room were watching for my world to turn upside down. Instead, they witnessed my world still in alignment with our Heavenly Father.

Many people believed that being away made the situation worse. Reflecting, I realized I needed to be away to hear God's voice. If I had been at home, I would have run somewhere. In Japan, I had no choice but to be still and know that God is still God.

I understood that whenever and wherever there's a crisis, Christ is.

The next day, an hour into my flight home, I remembered a letter Murice had written about a month prior. Murice was in the 3rd grade; he had a math test at school and received his 'A'. While he waited for his classmates, he wrote a letter to his father and me. He had never written us a letter before. Murice ran in the house shouting, "Mommy, Daddy, I wrote you a letter!" He not only expressed that he loved us, he also explained why he loved us, and wrote "*bye-bye*" at the end of all three pages.

The Thursday before their memorial service, I stood in my kitchen and prayed:

"*Dear God,*

Thank You so much for Murice's letter; it's the reason I can stand here right now. However, I need to know that Reggie was at peace. I need to know that he was also visited by the Holy Spirit."

I felt the Holy Spirit within me. I searched my home for over three hours and didn't find anything I prayed, trusted, and believed in.

Only as God can create it, only as God can orchestrate it. That evening was their school's open house. We went to Angela, Angelina, and Murice's classes, which were extremely emotional and healing. We finally made it to Reggie's second-grade class. Mrs. Blassey shared her tearful condolences.

Two weeks prior, Mrs. Blassey gave her students arts and craft supplies and said, "Do something for open house; your parents are coming!"

God designed this opportunity for Reggie to write his goodbye letter. Reggie cut out the shape of a house with closed doors. When I opened the doors, I almost fell to my knees. It was the letter I had searched for.

While I was writing my sons' memorial program, God revealed that their letters were written to soothe my soul, but more importantly, to share.

I served 15 years in the Air Force. I asked God if He would give me the strength to stay in the military for five more years, I would retire and dedicate my life to sharing His amazing testimony. God granted me that strength.

The scriptures that carried me were:

He gives us comforts in all our troubles. Then we can comfort other people who have the same troubles…
– 2nd Corinthians, 1:4

There's a time to weep, laugh, mourn, and dance.
– Ecclesiastes 3:4

I now share this testimony and support Christians overcoming grief so they can sing, laugh, and dance again.

Because peace is priceless, if you are grieving, please seek support. Your grief could be the transportation for your transformation.

You can read my full story in my autobiography, *Miracles in Action ~ Trusting God Through Your Storms*. From misery to miracles, from grief to peace, from storms to strength.

***

ANGELA ALEXANDER

MiraclesInAction.com

Bliss

Confessions of a Silver Lining Seeker

by Doreen Zimmerman

I live in Northern California as a nana, a mother, a writer, and an artist. After 47 years of marriage, I am learning what remains, and what becomes possible, when love outlives loss.

I had 47 years to accept the reality that one of us would have to die first. Forty- seven years to make peace with that truth. Somehow, it never quite took hold.

It has now been one year since my marriage ended, not because love did, but because life does. And when that moment arrived, I discovered that knowing something in theory is quite different from living it.

At that exact moment in my life, when theory became reality as it burst through my very core, I shook with disbelief. For so long, I fought the storm crashing upon our shore. With every fiber of my being, I fought the ebb, the pull, the taking away. When the tide came for Tod, I did everything in my power to stop it. I shook my fists, paddled like hell, screamed against the winds that came in with the tide. But nothing, not the doctors, not the research, not the tests or medicines, not even the love I held so fiercely, could stop it.

The tide was coming for him, no matter what I did. Desperately casting about for any port in the storm, I armed myself with every weapon I could muster. With love and care, I built dams and dikes that collapsed. With doctors and surgeries, I built bridges and detours that led us only back to where we had begun. I built as fast as I could, but the tide advanced steadily, relentlessly, as it has since the beginning of time. No matter how endlessly I cried, nothing could alter the destiny that awaited us. Acceptance became our only choice, and it was not a safe harbor.

And the tide came in. And it took him as it went out.

But it left me. Alone on this shore. Still standing. Fists clenched at my sides, empty, staring into the horizon where he disappeared.

It is a beautiful shore. Make no mistake about that. It is filled with our children and grandchildren underfoot, and with memories reflected in tidepools that shimmer with mercury-like wonder. These lightning-filled tidepools, constantly replenished by my tears, flash with fleeting moments of our life, where grief and beauty meet in concert.

Over time, I notice these tidepools are becoming rimmed with a silver lining so bright I can barely look into them. Staring into them sears my soul with bittersweet emotions, bringing me to my knees under a merciless force. They evoke a lifetime of love that lifts me into unbearable lightness, yet their very foundation rests on the truth that he is gone.

I am helpless, no, utterly incapable of looking away. I have developed a thirst for these bursts of light; they are a hot yellow-white-silver brilliance that blinds me as stars fill my eyes and heart. I have become a seeker of these silver linings. I am addicted.

And, as I stand on this shore, waves of the life we built take my breath away. I remember learning to drive in his '53 five-window Chevy, grinding the clutch to dust while he laughed and told me to try again.

I hear his calm voice guiding our family across a dangerous glacier, reminding us where to place our feet.

I see him laughing as the girls catch bait in the early Baja morning, the sun barely up, the smell of salt sharp in the air.

I feel his breath on my neck as he points out the Southern Cross in an Amazon midnight, his finger tracing a story across the sky.

I see us later, in years when we felt our time together was endless, giving freely and loving generously.

Standing here now, I have something I did not have for so many years during Tod's illness: unscripted time. Time without urgency. Time that is not dictated by survival. Time that stretches quietly in front of me, asking nothing. At first, that openness felt unbearable. Silence can be louder than chaos when you are used to constant caretaker motion.

There were days when the stillness pressed heavily against me, when grief threatened to fill every available space and convince me that this is all there ever will be. The illusion of having no choice shimmered in the distance like a mirage.

And yet, slowly, something else appeared beside it. Not instead of grief, but alongside it. A memory without pain. A laugh from another room. Sunlight warming my face in an early morning pause. These moments did not announce themselves. They were quiet, unassuming, and easily missed.

I began to understand that this shore was not a place of waiting, but of choosing. Life was still offering itself to me, not without loss, but honestly and without condition. The choice was not whether grief would exist, but whether I would allow it to eclipse everything else that remained. What would I choose? The realization that I had the privilege of this choice came tentatively, without confidence. But once seen, it could not be unseen. Something shifted. A subtle opening. Even here, after all that had been taken, I was still invited to participate in life. I could still choose. I still had the privilege of choosing a future filled with life and joy, if I so desired.

But whatever choice I made, other questions remained: *What is this blinding light that rims my tidepools of reflection? How incalculable was its worth?* These questions haunted me, as I stumbled through deep and unrelenting grief. The caretaker's sacrifice of self had dwelled deep and long inside of me, and it now mingled with the dark colors of loss and despair. It seemed as if grief was not only making it impossible for me to make a choice, but also to name and hold on to that brilliant silver lining.

And that silver lining was something to reach for and hold on to for dear life. And so I did.

I once thought of privilege as something external, something other people possessed. But when I flipped the script, it changed me. I began to see the life I had lived and the lessons it demanded as privileges entrusted to me. Even the hardest ones.

My hardest one? Holding my husband at the end of his life. It was neither fair nor easy. It was dark, murky, and devastating. But it was also a gift and a privilege. Not everyone is granted the gift of loving one person so deeply, or the privilege of standing with them at the threshold as their tide turns.

I realize, as I return to these tidepools of reflection, that all of life is a gift. All lessons, even the ones that break us open, are a privilege that carries a silver lining. I reflect on these tidepools, this light that frames my memories in the quiet of early mornings, and I think I see my future within. I believe there is clarity on the path I can choose going forward: this choice will not only cradle memories but, if I choose, can also reach, stretch forward, upward, onward, with joy and promise. This belief, this reflection of mine, makes me think that the silver lining in my tidepools . . . is me.

DOREEN ZIMMERMAN

Knowing Who We Are

by Cathy J. Yuhas

Finding Joy in Death Work: A Death Doula's Sacred Path

For many, the idea of finding joy while working in the realm of death may seem paradoxical. But for a death doula, joy is not only possible but also essential to the work. It is found in the deep connections formed with those facing their final moments, in the tenderness of holding space for grief and love to coexist, and in the profound awareness that life and death are part of the same sacred cycle. Death work is not about sorrow alone; it is about spirit, light, and the expansion of the heart that illuminates the beauty of existence.

The Power of Connection

At the heart of being a death doula is a connection: to the dying, to their loved ones, and to the universal experience of transition. One of the most profound experiences I've had as a death doula was with a childhood friend. She fought fiercely against her cancer, but it took its toll, and her spirit began to quiet. No one addressed the elephant in the room: she was declining at a rapid pace.

Her goal was to make it to her son's wedding, which was nine months away. We discussed stopping treatments that were having devastating effects and enlisting hospice's help, which would offer her a better quality of life and help her reach that goal more comfortably. After agreeing to that, she flourished. She felt physically better, could eat again, and her pain was under control. With that, she was able to connect more deeply with her friends and family.

When we connected, we shared our life adventures together, including our love of playing guitar, singing, and harmonizing. Sometimes, though, she expressed concern that whenever we got together, all we did was revisit the past and avoid necessary matters, such as arranging her affairs. To this day, I still chuckle inside because while reminiscing, she experienced such joy in those memories.

Although she didn't realize it, the conversations revealed to her that her life had meaning, which is crucial to coming to terms with the dying process. We shared laughter and warmth; I can still see her heart light up as she relived those cherished moments. For the dying, connection and knowing they are supported bring peace. Sharing memories and acknowledging life's meaning can provide immeasurable comfort. For me, the gift of this connection serves as a reminder of the sacredness of life itself. Every moment becomes a chance to deepen compassion, listen with an open heart, and honor the individuality of each person's journey. It's all about connections, between past and present, between souls, and between this world and whatever lies beyond.

Holding Space in the Heart

To truly hold space in our hearts for someone at the end-of-life means being fully present, witnessing without judgment, offering love without expectation, and allowing emotions to arise without fear or hesitation. Holding space does not involve fixing or changing anything; it means creating an environment where someone feels seen, heard, and safe to transition in the way that is right for them.

This sacred practice expands the hearts of the dying and the death doula. In sitting with another's mortality, I am reminded of my own; in doing so, I often experience a deepening of my own spiritual journey.

With my friend, holding space meant allowing her to have silence when she needed it, to speak when she was ready, and to simply "be." Some days, we sat together without words. Other days, she told stories of her youth, laughing at her misadventures, of which I was often a part. Holding space meant honoring whatever she needed at that moment.

Knowing Who We Are as Divine Beings

As a death doula, my work is deeply rooted in our understanding of who we are as divine beings. In the moments before death, many experience a shift: a softening, a surrender, an unspoken recognition that they are not alone. Whether through personal beliefs, sensing an ancestral presence, or something greater than ourselves, there is often an unshakable sense that death is not the end but a return to something familiar.

When my father was dying, I noticed a shift. As he drifted between wakefulness and sleep, he seemed to be conversing with someone. When asked who it was, he said he thought it could be his mother. Whoever he was communicating with, he nodded and sometimes let out soft giggles. It was as though he felt a quiet understanding. In that moment, I felt something too: a warmth, a sense that he was being held in something greater than we could see. Being a light in the sacred passage of death means recognizing these moments, honoring them, and allowing them to unfold without imposing meaning.

The Joy in Being a Witness to Love

Where there is death, there is love. In sitting vigil, comforting families, and honoring someone's last wishes, I witness some of the most heartfelt and sacred moments life has to offer. There is joy in seeing a family member finally speak the words they've held onto, in helping someone find peace with their past, and in watching love take center stage as all else fades away. In serving the dying, my heart expands. The work calls me to be more patient, more compassionate, and more attuned to what truly matters. What once seemed important fades in comparison to the profound presence needed in the moment of someone's passing. The heart stretches to hold not only the sadness but also the beauty of a well-lived life, a story well-told, and a departure from this world, embraced with grace.

This expansion is not only personal; it radiates outward, affecting the lives of others. By finding joy in death work, I help others do the same. I guide families to shift their perspectives from fear to acceptance, from uncertainty to trust, and from despair to meaning.

Bringing Light to the Final Moments

Ultimately, my role is to offer light, not by denying the weight of grief but by illuminating the love, connection, and meaning that still exists, even in the face of death. This light is found in how we listen, how we show up without hesitation, and how we remind others that no one should go through this journey alone.

There is joy in knowing that even in death, love remains. There is joy in being able to support another soul as they transition from this world, offering reassurance, compassion, and presence. There is joy in recognizing that by holding space for another, I also create space for myself to learn, grow, and honor the sacred nature of life itself.

With every death I witness, a palpable silence fills the room, creating a sense of mystery. Of course, there are tears, but there is also love. Within love, there is always joy. At its core, I see my work as a profound act of love. Love, like life, does not end; it simply transforms. After all, we are all just walking each other home.

❋❋❋

Cathy J. Yuhas, RN, CEOLD

Author of "Walking Each Other Home: Guiding Caregivers and Community Through the Sacred Passage of Death"

www.dyingmatters.llc
www.facebook.com/dyingmatters.ct

Step Seven: A Conscious and Compassionate World

Your Presence Creates Impact

> *"Human beings are deeply social. Acts of compassion and connection activate neural systems associated with empathy, trust, and cooperation. When we treat others with kindness and awareness, we strengthen the social bonds that support collective well-being. Compassion strengthens connection and emotional regulation." (Singer & Engert, 2019)*

You are not separate from the world. You are influencing it.

Your growth ripples outward.

Meditation: Remembering We Belong to One Another

Close your eyes.
Take a gentle breath in.
And slowly exhale.

Now bring someone you love into your awareness.

See their face.
Feel your connection to them.

Silently send them compassion. Peace. Understanding.

And now offer that same compassion toward yourself.

Because so often, we extend grace outward while withholding it inward.

Now allow that compassion to expand even further. Into your family. Your community. Humanity itself.

You see, creating a conscious and compassionate world does

not begin somewhere outside of us. It begins in the smallest moments.

The way we speak to one another.
The way we listen.
The way we choose understanding over cruelty.
The way we remain human in a world that sometimes encourages disconnection.

Human beings are profoundly interconnected. Research in social neuroscience continues affirming what wisdom traditions have long understood: we are wired for connection, belonging, empathy, and meaningful relationships.

We affect one another constantly.

A smile matters.
Presence matters.
Compassion matters.
Being witnessed matters.

And sometimes the smallest act of kindness becomes the very thing another person needed in order to continue.

Take another breath.

And quietly repeat:

"I choose compassion."
"I recognize our shared humanity."
"My presence contributes to healing."
"I bring awareness and kindness into the world."

And remember, we are all walking this earth together.

Moment by moment.
Choice by choice.
Human heart beside human heart.

> *"People have a tendency to think that the world owes them something or that people owe them something. But in reality, as we evolve, as we become more conscious, we discover that there is this Life Force or this Life Presence is seeking to become conscious of itself as us, according to our unique pattern."*

DR. MICHAEL BERNARD BECKWITH

MINISTER, AUTHOR, HUMANITARIAN, MUSICIAN
FOUNDER & SPIRITUAL DIRECTOR, AGAPE INTERNATIONAL SPIRITUAL CENTER

THE GIFT OF JOY

BY GAIA ORION

In the beginning, I painted simply because it gave me joy. It's a good reason to do art. Then, I saw fellow artists making a good living, and it inspired me to sell my paintings. I was the young parent of three babies, so no one around me thought it was a good idea. I don't blame them for trying to protect me from disappointment and poverty. Being a proud, stubborn, hard-working woman, I did not let discouragement from friends and family stop my ambitious vision.

For the past 25 years, I have led a professional art career like a kid dreaming big. I exhibit all over the world. I teach creativity to corporate and government institutions, and it's been a magnificent journey.

As I mature into an established artist, I realize that my drive to paint isn't just about joy and income. This process of creativity is taking me on a much deeper voyage. My symbolic, geometric, colorful images tell stories of the natural world and life cycles. They express the stages and states we go through as we unfold, grow and awaken. I paint the inner life, the invisible whispers of the heart, and the metaphysical nature of the universe.

Since I was a little girl, I've had a sense of wonder and awe for the mysteries of life. One day, my best friend, Constance, and I were gardening at a Girl Scout camp. As usual, we were chatting about big ideas: friendship, love, and God (I didn't know about the Goddess yet!). At one point in the conversation, we both started to cry uncontrollably. It's almost like we simultaneously experienced the vastness of life; it was too grand to hold as an idea, too big to comprehend. It felt as if our bodies and minds metaphorically exploded into pieces, and even though we were crouched with our hands on the earth, in that moment, we had lost touch with the ground. It was profound, mystical, and even though we were bawling our eyes out, it was a joyful experience we still talk about when we see each other.

Now in my fifties, I have enough years behind me to look at the essence of my life's trajectory. I always wanted to understand the meaning of life, unveil the secrets of the cosmos, and crack the code of daily appreciation, presence, and depth. That shared experience with my best friend at a young age became a beacon for my journey.

Knowledge of the deeper truth is not just expressed in the realm of words. That is why, instead of reading philosophers and sacred texts, I recount my quest into spiritual matters through art making. When I paint, I strive to transmit what lies beyond the veil of daily existence. I am aware that all this sounds a little serious. With everything, there is always the other side of the coin: Lightness! Humor! Joy!

Behind all these stern transcendental inquiries, I discovered that the juiciness of life lies in tiny moments of joy. It's not complicated at all. A cup of coffee while watching stand-up comedy, the smell of fresh-baked bread, the call of an owl across the river, the shimmering light on the water when the sun pierces through the clouds, a random smile with a stranger on the street, or a wink to a curious child in a stroller.

Joy is found through our senses, in our bodies, precious, miraculous vehicles that carry us through life.

It's when I am in touch with joy that my mind creates these mesmerizing images found in my art. Joy is the golden thread that ties earth and sky, body and spirit, outer and inner, matter and energy, reality and imagination. There is joy when I sketch, when I paint, and even more joy when I offer my art to the world.

Since early humans lived in caves, artists have enchanted lives with the beauty they create. They have transported people out of their daily drudgery, leaving them with offerings of goodness and truth. Laughing at a quirky theatre play, moved by the sweet characters in a movie, welling up with the climax of an orchestra, touched by the tender expression in a painting; art offers a direct portal to simple moments of joy.

You don't need to be an artist to discover the gift of joy that creativity gives. Anyone can experience it. Everyone has had access to it at some point in their life. Remember how easy it was, as a child, to feel a sense of lightness through creative activities? We all used crayons and paintbrushes, scissors and glue, wooden blocks, chairs, and sheets of paper to express whatever idea was rising within them. All of us played with sticks and rocks, climbed trees, and jumped in water, imagining worlds where we were superheroes and villains, kings and queens, dragons and elves.

You may say, "But I am an adult now; there is no place in my life for playing with fairies." One of the gifts of my life is that I get to hang out with a lot of artists. Our kind do not ask such questions! People are fascinated by artists because our minds create ludicrous formations, and nothing stops us when we decide to manifest them.

Have you been hiding in your heart and mind an idea or two that's a little crazy? Maybe it feels 'a little out there' because you see it in the context of who you have been until now. What if considering that creative thought could open a door to magical adventures? This proposition could be a way to discover the gift of joy in your life.

Let me take you there with a series of questions:

- What brought you the most joy when you were a child?
- Is there something you used to love doing but stopped because of a harsh comment from a parent, teacher, or friend?
- Is there one activity you could literally do all day, losing track of the clock and to-do lists?
- And how about that awesome idea you buried deep in your soul?

I invite you to journal with these prompts and see what emerges:

- Do you notice patterns?
- What surprises you most?
- How do you feel when you reread what you wrote?

Now look at the items that stood out. Start with something that feels in your reach and right to you.

- What is that small idea you could bring to life?
- Who do you trust most to share this idea with?

- What is the one action you could take to start moving toward that creative idea that brings you joy?

When all this feels too scary...

When you think, "This is just stupid."...

When you say, "It can't be for me."...

Remember: you are not alone on this journey.

When I started pursuing my dream of becoming an artist, no one I knew could see what I sensed was ahead of me. With each step I took to put my vision into motion, I met new people who were on that same path. Soon what I thought was crazy became another idea I was going to manifest. What was once a glimpse into what is possible became a reality, and much more. Little by little, my existence became that wondrous infinite world I had experienced with my friend sitting in a garden. I invite you to take your shoes off, feel the soft earth, and step on the path of limitless joyful creative potential! Life is awaiting you.

✵✵✵

GAIA ORION

www.gaiaorion.com
art@gaiaorion.com
@gaiaorionart (LinkedIn, Facebook, and Instagram)

Two Things

by Laurel Janssen Byrne

Two things can be true at the same time.

It is human nature to seek personal fulfillment and find the people and activities that make us happy and joyful in our lifetime. We read books, create art, travel, cook delicious food, laugh, and connect with friends. Our human experience is shared. We connect in our life's journey with one another, and we seek satisfaction.

Duality being what it is, light & dark, good & evil, female & male, right & wrong, the opposite is present also. Sometimes the negative energy of the world's chaos feels heavy and tragic. Yes, this is true. Darkness and those of malintent exist alongside us, and they are strong and greedy. And also, joy is among us, thriving in people with heartfelt intentions, and they are strong and generous.

You can find joy, experience joy, and immerse yourself in the pursuit of a joyful life. We cannot carry the weight of the world each day in our bodies, minds and souls. That would be crushing. Collectively, we must support each other and move forward with intention and goodness. That intention unlocks a new gear, resonating at a higher vibration, in the pursuit of joy.

Joy is so big, it's small.

I often write about my grandmothers. I was blessed with two marvelous grandmothers. One of them, Mavis, was a native Californian, raised on an orange ranch, a child of the Pacific Oce an, college educated, tall, strong, and kind. She taught me how to play cards, and to make a bed quickly and neatly. She gave me her copy of *The Complete Works of Shakespeare*, taught me how to make the best vinaigrette, and how to pot a roast. She was a great driver, teaching me all the back roads where she grew up, before the interstate highways were built. Practical and strong, Mavis possessed wonderful leadership skills and gave generously of her time and money. The other grandmother was a feisty redhead from Scotland, Annie, with her brogue and braids. She preferred the wonder of children to droll adult conversation, and despite her 8th grade education, knew more about nutrition and exercise than most people do today. She baked bread and sewed proficiently and was physically fit and sturdy. She laughed hard and walked briskly. She never drove a car but rather insisted on the importance of physical activity.

I loved them, and since they both lived into their 90s, I had them well into my own adulthood. They filled my childhood with countless happy moments, showing me the joy in their hearts.

Recently in my small town, I was racing around, running errands, busy with the tasks of my day. I was driving to the grocery store, talking to my mother on the phone, and just as I was about to hang up with her, I spied a wallet on the ground in the parking lot near my car. I hopped out to pick it up. It was a red wallet, zipped up neatly so nothing could fall out. I unzipped it to search for an ID. Its owner was a woman named Jeanette, and she was just a few weeks shy of her 91st birthday. Poor thing, I thought. This little old lady had lost her wallet and would be so nervous and upset when she realized it was missing. Her address was just a mile or so up my main road, so I hopped back in the car and headed to her home to return the wallet to her.

Upon my arrival to her little white & green house, a blooming yellow rose bush in front, a small lady was walking toward me down the driveway from the garage. Holding up the red wallet so she could see the reason for my unexpected visit, I said to her, "I believe I've found your wallet!" She raised her hands in relief, and joy spread across her face. "Oh, my goodness, I love you!" she exclaimed. And she threw her arms around my shoulders, giving me a hug of appreciation. "Wherever did you find it, dear?"

I told her the tale of her wallet in the grocery store parking lot. Laughing, she told me she was a silly old lady who carried too many things in her purse and must have dropped it. I said, "More annoying than losing your wallet is having to go to the DMV to replace your identification." If I had saved her that trip, my visit had been worth it.

And then I heard her brogue. When I mentioned it, she confirmed that she was from Glasgow but had lived in the US for many decades. Just like my own Scottish grandmother. Jeannette walked back up her driveway, her wallet safely tucked under her arm. Thanking me profusely, she waved good-bye to me.

We both left this interaction with smiles on our faces, faith in humanity restored, a joyful gear engaged. I headed back down the road to the grocery store and my errands of the day, lighter, joyful, filled with the simplest joy. Being able to help an old lady.

Hearing the voice of my grandmother's motherland. Helping someone. Such a small thing, yet also, so big. So very big, it's small. I like to think small acts of kindness and courtesy and consideration change the world. It's where I rediscover joy. Darkness may be growing as well, but two things can be true at the same time, and joy is growing every day, blooming in us.

***

LAUREL JANSSEN BYRNE is an author, editor, podcaster, and speaker.

She can be found on Amazon, Barnes & Noble, and on Instagram at @miss_laurel.

The Other Side of the Mountain

by Terree O'Neill

Gazing out my back window over the land I love, I feel gratitude swell through my heart. I am lucky to live in this mountain home, where my spirit has learned to soar again. Extending my arms outward, I breathe in the clear air and embrace the woman I have become. Richer from experience, more awake and aware of the fortunate place I occupy in this world, and desirous of living at each moment with infinite love and pure joy.

Hello, I am Terree O'Neill, a lover of life, a photographer and writer, sharing my story of loss and healing in the hope that my path to recovery is relatable to others who have lived through tragic events, and inspiring to those in the grip of painful experiences and on their own path of finding the light of life again.

My journey to this time and place began with tragedy, twice broken-hearted in a short span of time. When I look back toward the direction where it all happened, the places in my past, my physical view is blocked by the mountain on which I now live. The universe, I believe, wants me to know clearly that who and where I am now is a woman having lived through the pain, with the grief, to acceptance, healing, recovery, and peace. I continue to rebuild my life, with joy in my heart, one day at a time, on this other side of the mountain.

I marvel at the wonder of it all, having learned that what we need to heal is always available as long as we remain hopeful, open to possibility, and are willing to keep moving with our pain. As humans, our nature is to continue, and survival is our most basic instinct. That is what I did both times, instinctively survived the agony of losing my dear loved ones. I allowed myself to feel it all, to live the hurt, to enter the wound as often as I needed. I wanted to keep going and be strong for my family. Despite the hurt, I worked every day, looking for ways not to sink into despair, not to lose my own life in the process. Innately knowing I had to trust that I would figure it out, I grasped at straws, grabbed any lifeline I saw dangling, sang a song as a prayer a dozen times a day! Through the crippling pain of grief, an inner knowing that these terrible and tragic deaths would not defeat me, helped me to discover pathways to lighten my burden and continue living. These deep feelings pushed me to find my way after the first devastating loss, and again when the second unimaginable loss occurred.

My husband, Jake, my thirty-two-year companion and father of my three children, died after a brutal battle with cancer. His illness affected every aspect of the beautiful, full life we had built together. In an instant, with the words of a diagnosis and a rush to begin treatment, life as we knew it became a fight for his life. As a family, we did not think he would die; we believed he would heal and be healthy again. It only became brutally apparent that he would not survive when a group of doctors told me that there was nothing else they could do. Just three weeks later, Jake was gone.

His death was an immense loss to myself and my children, and the grief that descended on my life dominated every moment of every day that winter, into spring, summer, and fall. A relentless and intense storm struck me, leaving lasting wounds and altering my life significantly, none of which was within my control. The sadness, the anguish was unlike nothing I had ever experienced, and made the walls around me feel as though they were closing in. A year later, with a deep need to feel alive again, to become accustomed to being on my own, I set out on a faraway adventure. My heart needed healing, and my soul awakening, so I travelled to a place that lured me by its majesty and awe, Patagonia, an an exceptionally beautiful land in South America. The experiences with Nat Geo over three weeks of hiking glaciers and mountains, rounding Cape Horn by ship, and swimming in the Pacific Ocean off Easter Island, were akin to a rebirth. Exalted by wild beauty, I pushed myself beyond my physical limits and came away with a sense of accomplishment and a newfound confidence with which to move forward in my life.

Eventually I downsized my belongings, sold my home, and set forth on a new path for whatever was next...that is until just a few years later, my beautiful, amazing 28-year-old son Hunter lost his life. He died in a foreign country under mysterious circumstances. Shocking and devastating, this unbearable, searing pain took me to the floor and broke my heart completely. Shattered, I wondered how I could ever survive this crushing blow and how I could live without him.

Reflecting on those years now, I see myself doing everything in my power to keep going. The physical and emotional pain of losing Jake had been a sadness I eventually learned to live with, but losing my son, Hunter, has been an excruciating weight to carry and still takes enormous strength to bear. I held it together in work and social situations, but the moment I was alone, tears would begin to fall. Loudly sobbing, bellowing my son's name, "Hunter, Hunter, Hunter, where did you go? Why are you not here, how did you die? Oh, my son, how did this happen to you?!" My grief, present in every waking moment, separated me from life before. Feeling a great disconnect, I was living in a reality that was incredibly difficult to understand. How was it possible that my son was not coming back? After Jake died, the ache was brutal and sad, but it was the loss of my Hunter that cut the heart right out of my chest. I was thrown from the life I rebuilt into one of horrific pain, as though I was being gutted from the inside out. How I came to be a woman fully alive again with a heart full of love was through the power of connection, to others, to the natural world, and reconnecting with myself and all that I am.

It began with one of the passions of my life: the camera. Four months after Hunter died, I embarked on a photo project to learn how other mothers who had lost a child were able to survive and continue living life in any normal way. I met with these women, interviewed and photographed them. From this experience, I learned that love was a healer. The love these women had for the children and the ways they shared it outwardly to the world carried them along and permeated their existence.

I became friends with one of the participants in my project, Christina, who had lost her son, Josh, one year before Hunter died. She and I have since found ways to continue to honor our sons' memories together as we cherish our bond and friendship, a gift from our departed sons. A profound turning point for me occurred at a retreat Chris and I attended together. During an exercise based on the arc of suffering concept, we were instructed to physically stand in one of the following labeled areas: sunset, dusk, midnight, dawn, or daylight. Each label represented a phase of suffering from darkness into light. Of all those gathered in the room, it was my friend who was the only person standing in the daylight. Witnessing this, I was shocked yet overjoyed to learn that it was possible to be healed after such a brutal loss, to be able to experience joyfulness and have a full, rich life with acceptance and peace. Her standing in the daylight filled me with hope that one day I could find the light as she had!

I sought ways to be comforted, spending time around the mountain area in which I now live. Meeting people through community events, making photographs of the local beauty, and hiking the mountain trails nourished my wounded spirit, connected and grounded my soul. Being out in nature and spending moments in the forest began opening my heart wider, more than I realized was possible. Time in the great outdoors allowed contentment to begin filling my heart, and I noticed an uplift in the way I felt. To keep the momentum going, one summer day I ventured to a nearby lavender farm, Hope Hill, a name that resonated with me because it had to do with overcoming difficult life circumstances. There I wandered the lavender fields and immersed myself in the landscape, creating photos. Eventually I sat down on the grass to breathe in the wonder, and calming energy filled me, along with a hopeful beauty that gracefully warmed my heart.

Other humans are a gift, for they teach us how to be. People who had also experienced tragedy kept crossing my path, as if an external force were at play sending them my way. Learning the stories of what these individuals had been through connected me on a level in which I felt the hand of God upon me. It was love, and it was everywhere! I heard the universe letting me know

I was not alone, and I realized I could continue to live my life with a full heart. Becoming aware of others who had endured tragic loss, and seeing them live full, productive lives in peace, got me closer to my own healing, and helped me to understand that no matter what, life is beautiful.

When tragedy strikes, it is as if the entire world is suddenly at a distance, out there somewhere other than where you are. With sorrow as the nucleus, we are thrust into a space in which every moment revolves around the pain. Our survival instincts kick in and though we must feel all that the darkness brings, our humanness has already begun its healing journey. Reflecting on the moments when my family first experienced each loss, I found the cards, flowers, and heartfelt messages I received to be hugely significant. The presence of my family and the way friends showed up made me feel incredibly cared for. I saw the love for my husband, for my son, for my family, and I felt the love, and every ounce of it helped me along. Each act of kindness directed my way was like the kindling sticks used to build a fire. Over time the smolder became a flame, and the flames grew taller inside of me. The stronger the fire, the more energy I felt to push onward, to learn, to grow, to reconnect to life; my life and the rebuilding began again. I discovered that life is a beautiful gift. The more I unwrapped this idea, the better I felt for longer periods of time. Because I experienced how life slows when darkness descends, I now understand that I have the power to pause what I am feeling and immerse myself in the beauty of any moment. It always exists. It is always there. It just takes tapping into. Through loss and grief, through adversity, I have been given opportunities to connect more fully and love more deeply than ever before.

We need each other; we need the earth and all that exists around us and all that needs us too! Everything is speaking to us with meaning that can enrich our existence profoundly. We can learn, we can teach, we can share, and we can love. What an incredible gift!

I feel the sun rise over the horizon and light up my being with its radiant golden glow. The energy flows through me; my soul is singing with the glory of the morning. The song in my heart absorbs pleasure. I am one with everything and all is possible. I cherish the knowledge I discovered through loss and time. Our human existence is an endless opportunity for infinite moments of happiness, quietly alone or out in the world; we have the power to make it so. This beautiful, bountiful, magical life is all about love, and if we focus there, it expands with infinite possibility. With a heart full of desire to live my truth, connect with others, soak in the wonder, I am grateful beyond measure, and my intention is to share the love outward in every way I can on this, the other side of the mountain.

TERREE O'NEILL

Step Eight: Love

The Integration of Everything

> *"Love is the foundation that connects all of these principles. Experiences of love and compassion activate brain regions associated with trust, safety, and emotional connection. Love encourages openness, understanding, and meaningful engagement with life. Not as a concept. As a state of being. Love regulates the nervous system. Love creates safety. Love allows transformation."*
> *(Feldman, 2017; Porges, 2017)*

At the center of everything is love.

Love is what remains when alignment is present.

Meditation: Returning to Love

Close your eyes.
Take a slow, deep breath in.
And gently let it go.

At the center of everything is love.

Not performance.
Not perfection.
Not endlessly trying to earn approval or prove your worth.

But love as presence.
Love as connection.
Love as truth.

Place your hand gently over your heart and breathe.

There is a part of you beneath the conditioning, beneath the fear, beneath the defenses created through survival, that has always known how to love.

And perhaps that is what this entire journey has truly

been about.

Remembering.

Remembering your humanity.
Remembering your connection to others.
Remembering that love itself is omnipresent.

We see it everywhere.

In newborn children.
In nature.
In the instinctive way human beings reach for one another during pain, grief, joy, and celebration alike.

Love exists in the smallest moments.

In the way someone listens deeply.
In the way we begin again after disappointment.
In the way we continue opening our hearts despite everything we have lived through.

Research continues to affirm that love, belonging, emotional connection, and relational safety profoundly influence our mental, emotional, and physical well-being.

We are wired for connection.

Human beings heal through presence.
Through meaning.
Through connection.
Through love.

Take another breath.

And allow yourself to soften.

Not because life has been perfect.
But because your heart deserves peace too.

Quietly repeat:

"I am worthy of love."
"I give and receive love openly."
"Love exists within me and around me."
"I return to love again and again."

Rest here for a few quiet moments.

And when you are ready, gently open your eyes.

Bringing this love with you into your relationships, your work, your healing, and the world around you.

Because the truth is, the love you bring into this world matters more than you may ever fully know.

> *"It's the nature of the sun to do that. It doesn't withhold its shining, and it doesn't shine to get feedback. It just does it because that's its nature. When you're truly giving, versus giving for recognition, you're giving because you have to give. It's our nature to Love, it's our nature to express ourselves, it's our nature to give, and it's our nature to have fun and to play and to pursue things we're interested in."*

JACK CANFIELD

AUTHOR, SPEAKER, SUCCESS COACH, HUMANITARIAN, FOUNDER & CEO, CHICKEN SOUP FOR THE SOUL ENTERPRISES, INC.

ZEN OF JOY

BY PETER J. HUGHES

I am one who finds fulfillment when serving my purpose through teaching, leading workshops, directing stage productions, and working with clients. As an Intuitive and Spiritual Mentor, I am wired to recognize and nurture the Light in people, the Goodness, Soul and Humanity. Through storytelling, I extend a joyful invitation to explore, claim, and sustain our individual and collective higher potential. It is a privilege to witness people rewrite a story of limitation, break through walls of resistance, and step into a version of divine alignment not previously considered possible, yet always waiting to be claimed.

I invite you to consider the possibility that Joy is our birthright. The degree to which we are willing and able to experience Joy is our free will to choose. Our choice will never be judged by a most generous and loving Universe, which will always meet us where we are in our availability to align with Joy.

We will find Joy where we look for it. We will experience Joy where we are a match for it. We are much like transistor radios, in that if we are dialed up to KFEAR, and our Joy is broadcast on

KFAITH, all we are going to hear is static. Joy is a 24/7 broadcast. To dial up to this broadcast, we can shift the energy of our individual signal to align with the higher frequency of Joy. A first step in shifting our alignment toward Joy is to identify and course-correct our thoughts and beliefs about Joy as a birthright.

A most efficient and effective practice for honing our capacity for Joy is to acknowledge and nurture the things that are right in front of us that feed our spirit. Discovering bite-sized nuggets of Joy in practical and tangible ways, we create the habit of generating opportunities to attract and savor moments of Joy already within our reach.

I encourage you not to be deceived by the perceived simplicity of connecting with Joy in obvious places. Avoid getting bogged down in judging where you think Joy is worthy of being found. Joy is Joy–it doesn't have an attachment to where you find it. You could spend a year traveling the world in the pursuit of Joy and accomplish remarkably little. You could spend a Joy-filled moment appreciating a fresh set of flannel sheets on a cold winter's night and accomplish everything.

There is an expression: faith sees best in the dark. The same could be said about Joy. Tapping into Joy is easy when it's easy. However, when we find ourselves in the darker moments of the human experience, even the concept of Joy can appear to be beyond our reach.

I have navigated my share of walks through the dark side of the human experience, having hit rock bottom, lying bloodied and broken, knowing which way was up only because I had landed on my back. It is these dark moments which provide the contrast necessary to honor the soul lessons and soul agreements mapped out for us in our life's journey. This awareness doesn't make the darkness any easier or less painful to navigate. It does, however, bring purpose to the contrast. This awareness of purpose can feed our faith and lift us up through the contrast to rendezvous with Joy.

When we intentionally make ourselves available to align with Joy, whether we are experiencing Joy or the perceived absence of it, Joy will find us, often in what may seem the most unlikely of places, as was the case for me in the early stages of writing this chapter. Forty-eight hours after being diagnosed with inoperable liver cancer our precious dog, Zen, transitioned peacefully at home. My husband, myself, and Zen's buddy, Wish, were by his side. It was a deeply sad and profoundly sacred family experience. The three of us miss Zen terribly as we acclimate to the absence of his physical presence in our lives.

One evening, two-and-a-half weeks after Zen's transition, I was in our backyard making a trash bin run. Heading back toward the house, I was inspired to stop and take a moment to reflect. Pausing beneath the star-filled night sky I scanned the yard, remembering how Zen loved exploring for "treasures" during our quiet times gardening together.

My heart began to ache, and tears started to well up. Then I spotted some movement out of the corner of my eye. Turning to see what it was, I was met by the image of Zen coming out of the house through the dog-door, stopping, then raising his nose and sniffing the night air. I walked over to the spot where he always stood during these scanning sessions, and said, as was part of our routine, "Hey, sweet boy, what are you picking up?"

Suddenly, I felt a wave of energy moving up behind me. I turned to find the spirits of dozens and dozens of dogs walking out from the shadows of the gardens onto the moon-lit yard. I turned to Zen, who was now wearing the most beautiful dog smile across his precious face. "These are my friends," he announced. "I invit ed them here to play. Is that okay?" Turning back to the onslaught of guests, I found the yard now filled with a hundred of Zen's new friends. All sizes and breeds, ages and markings, each with a distinct personality, all of them projecting that glorious, unconditional love we experience with our canine soul mates.

"Of course!" I said without hesitation, my arms opening wide to welcome the pack. "Absolutely!" Zen was happy, so happy, and he wanted to share his happiness with me. That was the way he was in life and how he will always be in spirit. Once again, I found myself overcome with emotion. However, this time, the tears were informed by a heart full of Joy.

Soaking in the energy of the one hundred dog spirits, I felt bubble-wrapped in the Love that Zen was in our lives, and the Love he will always be in our hearts. I believe Love is Zen's gift to us, his legacy. And we have an in-spirit dog park in our backyard to remind us of how loved we are. Walking back into the house, the smile on my face matched the Joy in my heart.

The value of allowing ourselves to experience Joy while we are navigating deep grieving is the healing Light that Joy brings to the grieving process. Joy lights the path along life's journey, so we may stay the course to the healed version of ourselves the grief is intended to facilitate. Grief is not a destination, but rather a soul-expanding process. Embracing moments of Joy while we are grieving realigns us with the Love that is our eternal Divine Truth.

I like to think the Final Judgement we anticipate encountering at the end of our life experience goes something like this: Standing before Divine Source, before God, our all-Loving Creator, we are asked one question, "Now, are you willing to see and experience yourself as I see and experience you … with Love, in Love, as Love?"

❋❋❋

PETER J. HUGHES is an author, life-shift facilitator, stage director, and advocate for reclaiming our humanity.

www.peterjhughes.com

Peace as the Pathway to Joy

by Robin Duncan

There are moments in life when the ground beneath you gives way, not all at once, but slowly enough that you don't notice until you can no longer stand on what once felt solid.

From the outside, my life appeared stable and successful. I had built a long career in finance as a CPA and CFO. I understood strategy, planning, and control. I believed that if I thought carefully enough and worked hard enough, I could solve whatever life placed in front of me.

What I did not yet understand was that no amount of careful thinking can anticipate every challenge. Life has a way of revealing that even the most carefully constructed plans can shift–and sometimes fall apart.

When the structures I relied on began to collapse, I did what I had always done: I tried harder. I searched for answers, strategies, and solutions. Eventually, my efforts stopped working. I found myself standing among the broken pieces of a life I could not fix, and for the first time, I was willing to admit a simple truth:

I did not have the answers.

That admission became the turning point, not because clarity arrived immediately, but because I became willing to release my resistance to being helped. In that willingness, I discovered something astonishing: divine help had always been available, patiently waiting for my invitation.

That willingness opened the door to an unexpected inner journey, one that carried me from numbers and strategy into deep healing and revelation, and eventually, into mentoring and lecturing on the principles of *A Course in Miracles* and the spiritual awakening that comes from reconnecting with God. Along the way, I learned something simple yet life-changing:

When peace becomes the goal, joy follows naturally.

When Happiness Gives Way to Despair

For most of my life, I was genuinely a happy person. Yet happiness did not always extend to my circumstances, relationships, or work. Joy appeared only in brief glimpses.

Then everything fell apart.

Within the same month, my marriage ended, and I was laid off from my position as a CFO. These were not merely external losses; they dismantled the internal structures I had relied on for identity, stability, and meaning. What followed was not ordinary sadness, but a dark night of the soul.

Whatever trace of happiness I had known was uprooted and replaced with despair.

Despair settles in when the future feels uncertain, and the past no longer makes sense. In that space, happiness feels unreachable, and joy seems meant for some other life entirely.

I wasn't chasing happiness. I was simply trying to survive: protect my children, navigate the pain, and find my footing again.

Choosing Peace as the Goal

Through *A Course in Miracles*, I encountered an idea that quietly redirected my healing: instead of trying to solve every problem or control every outcome, make peace the goal. When peace is the goal, the Teacher of Peace within you can show you the way.

So, I made a quiet decision, not once, but many times a day, to let peace be my goal.

Instead of *how will I pay my mortgage?* I chose; *my goal is peace.*

Instead of *how will I find a new job?* I returned to the same choice.

Each time I did, the Teacher of Peace within me offered the next step, not all the steps, just the next one. I learned to pause and listen for guidance that felt peaceful and compelling before taking action, trusting this inner voice.

That decision marked the beginning of a healing journey, not one I orchestrated, but one I was gently led through.

Listening to the Teacher of Peace Within

When peace is your goal, something remarkable happens. You align with the Teacher of Peace within you, and this wiser voice becomes easier to hear, not loud or dramatic, but steady, kind, and clear.

Guidance may arrive as a quiet thought, a gentle nudge, a line from a book or song, a message from a friend, or an unmistakable inner knowing.

I came to understand this Teacher as the part of us that never decides against ourselves, others, God, or our own happy outcome. This voice never shames, rushes, or threatens. It gently guides us away from fear and back to peace.

Listening required humility. I had to stop insisting that I already had the answers and release judgments, especially those I held against myself. The Teacher of Peace never led me through force, only gentleness.

The Path Was the Healing

There was no single realization that changed everything overnight. Healing unfolded slowly, through ordinary moments and repeated choices.

Guided by peace, I learned how to:

- Pause and ask for guidance instead of reacting
- Question fearful thoughts rather than believe them
- Release self-judgment
- Stop attacking myself or others internally
- Trust peaceful guidance instead of control

Each step toward peace softened something inside me. And in that softening, joy began to emerge, not as an achievement, but as a natural state.

Joy returned the way it always does: quietly and without fanfare.

Joy Is Not Created, It Is Uncovered

One of the greatest misunderstandings about joy is the belief that it must be achieved. Joy does not need to be manufactured, as it already exists within you.

Joy lives beneath layers of fear, grief, worry, and self-doubt. As these layers dissolve through peace and gentle guidance, joy naturally rises to the surface.

This is why peace is such a powerful pathway to joy. When you invite peace and allow divine wisdom to guide you, you are given exactly what you need, step by step. Once peace is established, joy follows naturally as an added gift.

I have learned that when you ask for and accept divine guidance, success is assured, and it always comes with a bonus.

The bonus is joy.

Sharing What You Learn Multiplies Joy

Another truth revealed itself along the way: joy deepens when it is shared.

As I began to write, speak, and support others from a place of peace, joy expanded within me. As *A Course in Miracles* teaches, when you are healed, you are not healed alone. Giving and receiving are not separate, they are the same movement of grace.

Practical Steps for Those Who Feel Far from Joy

If joy feels distant, here are gentle truths I've learned firsthand:

1. **Be willing to forgive whomever you are judging.**
   Forgiveness makes room for peace, and willingness is always met with help.

2. **Do not aim for joy if it feels impossible; aim for peace.**
   Peace is the doorway joy walks through.

3. **Listen inwardly before reacting outwardly.**
   Release judgment and follow what feels peaceful and compelling.

4. **Do not decide against yourself. Choose again.**
   Ask gently, w*ill this lead me toward peace or away from it?*

5. **Stand firmly on your goal of peace.**
   Pause frequently, step back, and allow guidance to show you the way.

A Joy-filled Life Is Possible

I did not find joy by trying harder. I found it by releasing the obstacles I had placed in front of it. Through gentle guidance, I learned to ask for help, release judgment, and remain committed to peace.

As peace grew, joy followed, abundantly and unexpectedly.

A joy-filled life is not reserved for a few. It is possible for anyone willing to choose peace and allow themselves to be guided by the highest place of wisdom within, waiting eagerly for a sincere invitation.

❋❋❋

ROBIN DUNCAN

For additional tools, reflections, and gentle support as you continue your journey toward peace and joy, you are welcome to explore the resources available at **RobinDuncan.com.**

A Daily Prayer for Peace and Joy

Take a moment to pause.
Let your body soften.
Let your breath slow.

You may read this silently or aloud:

Today, I choose peace as my goal.
I release the need to figure everything out.
I am willing to be guided instead of controlled by fear.

I invite the Teacher of Peace within me to decide for me.
Help me see this moment differently.
Help me release judgment, especially the judgments I hold against myself.

Where I feel uncertain, bring clarity.
Where I feel afraid, bring gentleness.
Where I feel blocked, open a way I cannot yet see.

I do not decide against myself today.

I choose peace, and I trust that joy will follow.

And so it is.

Sit quietly for a few moments after reading.
Notice what feels calmer, softer, or lighter, even slightly.

You do not need to force joy.
You only need to offer peace a home.

Accessing Joy

Thank you for aligning with us. You've now experienced many versions and pathways to joy in work, life, and relationships. Joy is the emotion that is brought up in you by success, well-being, or good fortune. It is a delightful feeling that is expressed as this. It is a mode or state of being in bliss, happiness, or felicity. Now you know that joy can reside in you. It can be brought up constantly and consistently when you think of what you're grateful for. It can be experienced and expressed concurrently with sadness, anger, or frustration. It can be brought with you or found at work; it can add so much value to relationships, and it can uplift your life overall.

Now that you have discovered how to experience joy, you are aware of it. Having this awareness creates an opportunity to leave space in your life for the joy to flow in or to be brought up. You can let go of negative people, habits and activities that drain you, things that feel forced or the "shoulds" that you have and begin adding in those positive practices of what elevates you that can spark joy into your world. You can cultivate joy by being in the positive habit of noticing it. It helps to speak it out loud, write it in your journal, or even keep a jar where you keep track of joyful experiences in your home.

Joy is a valuable currency. You get to share it with others and help them become joyful too. It is a gift you receive just by being alive. You can truly experience it in all that you do, and we celebrate this and feel a strong sense of gratitude for what the universe provides. It helps us understand why we are here and realize that life is like a wonderful journey with color, music, magic, and energy. It is pure joy.

– KIM SOMERS EGELSEE

Conclusion

You have arrived here, not by accident, not by chance, but by the quiet, steady unfolding of your own life.

Every page you turned, every moment you paused, every reflection that stirred something within you: it has all brought you to this place of awareness. And now only one question remains.

What will you do with what you know?

Because you already know. There is a part of you that has been listening all along, a part that recognizes truth when it is felt, a part that does not need permission to step forward. It has been here the whole time.

Insight

It may come as a whisper, a knowing, a feeling you cannot quite explain and yet cannot ignore. Honor it. Let it be enough. Your insight does not need to be decoded. It is already pointing you home.

Intention

From that place, you are invited into intention. Not as a distant goal, but as a living choice made in this very moment. You do not need to see the entire path. You only need to take the next step. Intention is not a plan. It is a declaration of who you are choosing to be.

Integrity

As you step forward, you are called into integrity. To live what you know. To align your actions with your truth. To stand in who you are, especially in the quiet moments when no one else is watching. This is where trust is built, not only with the world around you, but within yourself.

You do not walk this path alone.

Involvement

The way you show up in your relationships. The way you listen. The way you care. The way your presence shifts the quality of a room. You contribute to the lives of others simply by being fully here. Your presence matters more than you may ever fully realize.

And over time, something beautiful begins to happen.

Integration

Your insight, your intention, your integrity, your involvement are no longer separate. They become a way of living. Not perfection. Not some fixed destination you arrive at and leave behind. But a continual returning. A steady, grounded way of being that allows you to move through life with clarity, compassion, and truth.

You are not becoming the gift.

You are remembering that you already are.

And as you live from that place, something shifts within you and around you. Like a stone placed gently into still water, your life creates a ripple. It moves outward in your words, in your choices, in the quality of presence you bring into every room you enter.

You may not always see it. But it is felt.

You are felt.

Life is not waiting for you somewhere in the distance. It is here, in this breath, in this moment.

If this work has offered you anything, let it be a return to what already lives within you. To listen to your insight. To follow your intention. To live with integrity even when no one is watching. To stay meaningfully involved in what matters most. And to integrate it all, again and again, as a way of being.

None of it exists in isolation. It moves as one. Just as you do.

Take a breath. Let it fill you. And release it completely.

You are seen.

You are valued.

You are needed.

You are loved.

And your life, just as it is, carries meaning.

Move forward with that. With love. With grace.

With the quiet strength of someone who knows that what they bring to this world matters.

Because it does. It always has. It always will.

It's Why We're Here

– Shajen Joy Aziz, M.Ed., M.A.

References

APA Style — Blended

Davidson, R. J., & Begley, S. (2012). The emotional life of your brain. Penguin.

Davidson, R. J., & McEwen, B. S. (2012). Social influences on neuroplasticity. Nature Neuroscience, 15(5), 689–695.

Doidge, N. (2007). The brain that changes itself. Penguin.

Fredrickson, B. L. (2001). The role of positive emotions in positive psychology. American Psychologist, 56(3), 218–226.

Ryan, R. M., & Deci, E. L. (2001). On happiness and human potentials. Annual Review of Psychology, 52, 141–166.

Seligman, M. E. P. (2011). Flourish. Free Press.

Southwick, S. M., & Charney, D. S. (2012). Resilience: The science of mastering life's challenges. Cambridge University Press.

Tedeschi, R. G., & Calhoun, L. G. (2004). Posttraumatic growth. Psychological Inquiry, 15(1), 1–18.

Recent Research (2024–2025)

Recent neuroimaging reviews on emotional well-being and brain function (2024–2025).

Recent mindfulness and neuroplasticity systematic reviews (2024).

Recent resilience and prefrontal regulation frameworks (2025).

Recent qualitative research on joy and meaning-based well-being (2025).

Recent studies on compassion, connectedness, and the social brain (2025).

www.ingramcontent.com/pod-product-compliance
Lightning Source LLC
LaVergne TN
LVHW020709110826
845149LV00012B/2175
9798995496410